D0929183

Better Giving

Also by George G. Kirstein

Stores and Unions
The Rich: Are They Different?

Better Giving

THE NEW NEEDS OF
AMERICAN PHILANTHROPY

George G. Kirstein

HOUGHTON MIFFLIN COMPANY BOSTON 1975

Library of Congress Cataloging in Publication Data
Kirstein, George G.   Better giving.
Bibliography: p.   Includes index.
1. Endowments — United States. I. Title.
HV91.K53   361.7′6′0973   75–12562
ISBN 0–395–20711–8

Printed in the United States of America

w 10 9 8 7 6 5 4 3 2 1

Dedicated to

my sister, Mina Curtiss, and my brother,
Lincoln Kirstein, who taught me more about
philanthropic priorities than I learned
from my other research.

Acknowledgments

DURING MY LIFETIME I have had the privilege of sitting on the boards of trustees of two voluntary hospitals, two educational institutions, one agency concerned with the blind, one ballet company, and one foundation which distributed millions of dollars to philanthropic causes. From my fellow trustees and the professional staff members of these institutions, I learned much about the problems of fund raising and fund allocation.

In doing the specific research for this book, I talked to and corresponded with literally hundreds of individuals. I am grateful to every one of them who gave up valuable time to share expert knowledge. Many of their suggestions recommended books, articles, or pamphlets on their special fields. The unfailing efficiency and courtesy of the librarians at the Mamaroneck Free Library, headed by Mrs. Sally Poundstone, made it possible for me to have access to whatever volume I required. Whenever the rather modest collection of this village library did not possess a required book, it was borrowed from some other library that had it.

The following men agreed to read chapters in draft form and gave me the benefit of their criticism: Dr. George Silver of the Yale School of Public Health read the chapter on the health agencies; Mr. Mo Katz, Deputy Director of Montefiore Hospital and Medical Center, read the chapter on hospitals; Messrs. Jacob Trobe, Director of Jewish Child Care Association of New York, Joseph B. Gavrin, Executive Director, New York State Council of Voluntary Child Care Agencies, and Joseph H. Reid, Executive Director, Child Welfare League of America, read the chapter on children. I am grateful to each of them; however, from the acidity of some of their comments on my various conclusions, it should be made clear that the finished work in no way reflects their views.

Two people were of particular assistance. Over a five-year period my former colleague, Carey McWilliams, editor of *The Nation*, sent me a continuous flow of clippings and articles concerning different facets of the subject. As Mr. McWilliams appears to read everything printed in this country, his assistance was invaluable. Mrs. Joyce Hartman, my editor, was always encouraging and helpful, and her advice and criticism improved the book.

Finally, Mrs. Laura Jensen, my secretary, who has typed so many drafts of various sections that she must be heartily sick of the whole subject, has earned my continuing respect and gratitude.

Contents

x   *Contents*

Introduction

WHEN WE EXAMINE our social institutions, we frequently find that the popularly accepted image does not accurately reflect reality. Our politics, for example, are neither as pure as civics textbooks describe them, nor quite as dirty as muckraking journalists, searching for a sensational story, portray them. Our voluntary philanthropic institutions mirror a generally flawless image of social worth, human dedication, and virtue that is almost unique in our disillusioned and increasingly cynical society.

The image's glow is not hard to explain. What intrepid crusader would be foolhardy enough to mount an attack against the Red Cross? Or the Girl Scouts? Or the Salvation Army? Or the American Cancer Society? Or the United Funds? Or, for that matter, any of the more than 100,000 other honorably conducted, "do good" philanthropic agencies that exist today in the United States? These outlets for human compassion, these voluntary responses to human needs, these repositories of surplus wealth and recipients of excess income, are virtually invulnerable to general criticism.

Who can possibly be damaged enough by these institutions to justify complaint? No one is forced to contribute to them. They are voluntary. Nor is anyone required to accept their beneficences. Their good deeds are not mandatory, as are kindred government programs designed for the alleviation of social ills. Furthermore, it would be difficult if not impossible for even the most confirmed sceptic to find a philanthropic agency that does not do at least some good.

Quite apart from the absence of criticism, there exists a considerable vested interest in maintaining the purity of the image. Millions of people, no one knows precisely how many, work either as paid employees or as volunteers for the multitude of agencies which dot America. Twenty-one of the largest philanthropic agencies alone attracted volunteer work from over 43 million individuals in 1973. In addition, donors to these worthy causes, for their own ego satisfaction as well for the well-being of the agencies, must remain convinced that their contributions are well spent. In 1973, the total of philanthropic gifts by all Americans to all causes exceeded $24.5 billion. And this huge figure grows larger each year.

The following table demonstrates the trend in the last decade:

The Growth of Philanthropy 1963-72[1]

Year	Total Giving (billions)	Year	Total Giving (billions)
1963	$10.67	1968	$16.81
1964	11.44	1969	18.58
1965	12.21	1970	19.30
1966	13.89	1971	21.29
1967	14.77	1972	22.68
		1973	24.50

Unless the current recession combined with inflation reverses this trend, the $25 billion level in total giving will be surpassed in the near future.

Looking at only one segment of this vast total presents dramatic evidence of the postwar philanthropic boom. Between 1940 and 1958, contributions to just voluntary health and welfare agencies operating at either the national, regional, or local levels increased more than sevenfold, from $188 million to $1.5 billion.[2] In the next decade, 1958 to 1968, a period of almost uninterrupted prosperity, contributions multiplied by another three times, and agencies in these fields represented only one quarter of total philanthropic giving.

The belief is widely held that donations by the rich play the major role. The facts, as nearly as they can be adduced, paint a somewhat different picture. In 1969, according to Internal Revenue statistics, people with incomes under $15,000 gave $314 on the average for a total of $3.14 billion. Even those with incomes under $5000 gave a total of some $800 million. No doubt much of this money was donated in small sums, perhaps put in the collection plate at Sunday church services. Of course, those with incomes above $15,000 contributed a greater total of $6 billion. In 1970, the latest year for which complete figures are available, some 35 million citizens reported their specific philanthropic gifts to the Internal Revenue Service. Another 40 million citizens, nearly all with incomes under $10,000, filed non-itemized tax returns, and it is estimated that they contributed some 1.4 billion philanthropic dollars for a grand total in 1968 of $12.6 billion. This large sum proves beyond question that participation in philanthropy is not limited to the rich; all but the poor give varying sums. By 1972, Internal Revenue estimated that the total given by individuals had risen to $16.91 billion.

Quite apart from the magnitude of the funds involved, the worthy objectives of thousands of philanthropic agencies inhibit any harsh examination. Religious causes receive nearly one half of all philanthropic donations. Education gets about 16 percent, and health and hospitals receive only slightly less. While the arts, humanities, and cultural causes in general receive a far smaller percentage, total gifts to endeavor in these fields come close to a billion dollars a year. Who but the confirmed misanthrope would find fault with the general aims of religion, of education, of health agencies seeking the cure for disease, of hospitals, or of cultural institutions encouraging the arts?

Yet the image is not quite a true reflection of reality. Diligent fund raisers seeking support for their favorite causes use such phrases as "help the needy," "give to the less fortunate," and "remember the poor." The word "charity" is used as a synonym for "philanthropy." The reality is that charity in the sense of almsgiving to the poor has virtually ceased since government has established relief measures, inadequate as they may be, for the indigent. The reality is that the middle class benefits far more from the fruits that fall from the philanthropic tree than do the poor. Whether we consider the Boy Scouts, Harvard University, centers for the performing arts, America's voluntary hospitals, or most of the vast number of agencies pleading with outstretched hands for the philanthropic dollar, the poor receive surprisingly little from voluntary funds.

The image presented by philanthropic institutions, be

they museums or social work agencies, hospitals or colleges, botanical gardens or opera companies, reflects endeavors presided over by distinguished citizens who devote considerable time to the close supervision of their favorite organization. The image accurately reflects reality in that most philanthropic boards of trustees are composed of distinguished citizens, but after that, image and reality part company. The self-selecting, self-perpetuating, undemocratic boards of trustees in a vast number of cases exert little control over the institutions they oversee, meet infrequently, are in fact rubber stamps for paid administrators, and in some cases are hardly aware that they are members of the boards of agencies which proudly list their names on the letterheads.

The image reflects generous donors, prompted by compassion for the plight of those less fortunate, who willingly sacrifice their own needs to help others. Here again reality is not at the opposite pole, for no doubt there are many individuals who fit this description. There are also a great many who give reluctantly because their employer, or supervisor, or foreman makes it clear that their company frowns on those who do not contribute their "fair share" to the United Fund, and in many instances the reluctant donor is told precisely what his "fair share" is to be. Others are prompted to be "generous" because of tax considerations. Still others adopt a charitable cause because the social events sponsored by that organization provide favorable contacts for upward mobility within the social fabric of their community. It is not unknown for people to give to philanthropy out of hatred, in order to deny funds to an unfaithful wife or an ungrateful child. Words such as "generous," "sacrifice," "humanitarian," and "public-spirited" are bandied about in connection with large gifts to worthy causes, but these phrases more accurately acclaim the magnitude of the donations rather than the motives which prompted them.

The generally accepted impression, one which is embellished by fund-raising appeals, encourages the belief that if donors do not give generous support, the cure for cancer will not be found, hospitals will close, and a huge diminution of effort will result as the institutions are forced to depend on the meager handouts from government. Truth is that government spends $10 for every single philanthropic dollar in the joint search for the causes and cures of the diseases that afflict us. Furthermore, government shoulders the lion's share of the burden in child care, care of the sick, education, and many of the other social services. Only in the arts and purely cultural activities is the philanthropic contribution far greater than government's, and even in these areas, government's share is steadily rising.

The popular belief is that the magnitude of philanthropic effort in any particular direction bears a direct relationship to the urgency of the needs. The facts are that the emotion-stirring fund appeal and the efficiency of the soliciting organization determine the magnitude of the effort. For example, nearly four times as many people suffer from heart ailments as from cancer, but the American Cancer Society's annual take is $65 million whereas the American Heart Association's is $45 million. The Muscular Dystrophy Association of America raises more money (nearly $10 million) than the National Multiple Sclerosis Society ($7.5 million), although two and a half times as many people suffer from sclerosis as from dystrophy. The National Foundation (March of Dimes) in its heyday was by far the most heavily supported agency in the medical care field, although — fortunately — polio afflicted only one out of every 30,000 Americans.

Finally, donors have a right to believe that once a crusade to which they contribute is won, the solicitations will cease and their gifts can benefit a new cause. But history fails to support this faith. Once a philanthropic agency has established a successful fund-raising organization, it is virtually immortal. The March of Dimes was formed to wipe out polio, but although Salk vaccine and other remedies accomplished this purpose, the dimes keep marching, albeit in a new direction. The Child Labor Committee was established to eliminate the curse of children's toiling in factories, but once the Child Labor Law, which terminated this abuse, was passed, the worthy organization about-faced and set up a program to find jobs for young people. Given steadfast support, objectives become flexible.

The task of establishing an accurate picture in the field of philanthropy is not easy. Authorities or even knowledgeable participants in a particular philanthropic activity are reluctant to voice any criticism which might dam up the flow of dollars to their favorite cause. Millions of well-intentioned people prefer to believe in the illusion rather than examine the facts. But as in all other endeavors, truth is the path to wisdom, and the human struggle toward perfection demands the emergence of harsh reality over a pleasant image.

Better Giving

CHAPTER 1

Giving—The Golden Crowbar

MAN, LIKE ALL OTHER ANIMALS, places his highest priority on individual survival. If others possess what he needs to survive, he will try to take it from them by force, by stratagem, or by theft. However, once his survival is assured, reasoning man, unlike the other animals, is willing to share his surplus with his neighbors. As civilization developed and man achieved not only survival but even various degrees of comfort and affluence, his willingness to share increased and was counted a virtue. By the time man had adopted the concept of some form of life of the soul after death of the body, the good deed of sharing with neighbors or, more formally, giving to charity became a symbolic golden crowbar which helped to force open the gates of heaven.

Organized philanthropy establishes one method of coping with the shortcomings of modern society, while furnishing a convenient recipient for people's various compulsions to give. Since Biblical times, giving to the poor has been considered praiseworthy, and the belief has prevailed that a man's sins could be expiated, even during his lifetime, by donation. Many motives besides generosity prompt giving, and because this human urge sustains the huge economic activity of American philanthropy, it is important to recognize at least a few of the many impulses which generate this largess.

The analysis of a scholar studying the motives of the eighteenth-century philanthropists in England still applies today:

> One finds mingled in variable proportions the impulses of religion, humanitarianism, vanity, social responsibility, malice, determined (and often bigoted) convictions on some special question, or the simple puzzlement of testators who lacked close relatives.[1]

An English author sought an explanation from orthodox psychiatry:

> Generosity could reflect some more or less pathological craving for status or power. It could be a neurotic attempt to buy reassurance and even love, or to create the illusion of involvement with the world while avoiding the challenge of real, direct relationships.[2]

An American psychologist offers a more cynical explanation:

> In one way or another, instead of feeling humility and being grateful for being given a chance to pay back our debt to humanity, the true factor that is involved is, "I am capable of giving money." That's only one side of the coin. There's a much more serious one, an unfortunate side: That by *not* giving money, I can play God just as well. "I could give to you; you keep on begging me, keep on asking me — I just won't."[3]

An economist, employing his discipline to explain philanthropy's golden flow, wrote:

> It is tempting for the economist to argue that there are really no gifts and that all transactions involve some kind of exchange, that is, some kind of *quid pro quo*. If we drop a dime in the blind man's cup, it is because the blind man gives us something. We feel a certain glow of emotional virtue, and it is that we receive for our dime. Looked at from the point of view of the recipient, we might suppose that the blind man gives out a commodity or service which consists in being pitiable.[4]

A philosopher translates the exchange theory into religious terms:

> Does not the Christian depend for his salvation on the beggar? No beggars, no Christian charity.[5]

The attachment of donors' names to imposing buildings or institutions confirms the exchange theory. Duke, Vanderbilt, Carnegie-Mellon, and Stanford are only a few of the educational institutions with designations memorializing their benefactors. Walk across nearly any campus and the names of donors, carved in imperishable marble, will greet you from the portals of many buildings. In the same way, the component parts of great medical complexes are individually identified by the names of donors, past or present, who supported their construction. Enter the hospital and you will find operating rooms similarly labeled, wards with plaques commemorating donors, even small plates over individual beds memorializing less affluent benefactors. Prestigious prizes — Nobel, Pulitzer, Lasker — continue annually to remind us of men long dead. Professorships and scholarships as well bear the names of those who endowed them. As for the reason givers so commonly request this recognition, we can only assume that it is the desire not so much for present approbation as for future appreciation. The bronze plaques and the stone carvings assure far longer memories than a current newspaper story announcing the gift.

No one can say precisely whether these name-attached gifts demonstrate a quest for immortality, praise, gratitude, or just recognition, but we do know that relatively few donations are made anonymously. According to estimates, fewer than 10 percent of large gifts come from unidentified sources, and certainly fund raisers for colleges, hospitals, or museums would feel totally frustrated if they were instructed to seek only anonymous gifts.

Often the negative emotion of fear plays a positive role in swelling the flow of gifts. In the past few years, for instance, large numbers of whites, appalled by the specter of fire, looting, and violence in the ghetto rioting of successive long hot summers, contributed money to causes dedicated to improving the position of blacks. The sniper fire and explosions of Molotov cocktails within a few miles of comfortable middle-class homes posed a threat to a way of life. Tranquillity, if not contentment, had to be restored, and philanthropic appeals to help the blacks toward equality contained the implicit threat that, unless gifts were forthcoming, dangerous violence would continue. (Some militant black spokesmen recognized this motivation and contemptuously referred to the resulting programs as "pacification.")

Some of the large philanthropic health agencies have long recognized the efficacy of frightening people to loosen their purse strings. Perhaps organizations to combat cancer offer the best examples of the use of fear in public education and fund-raising campaigns, but agencies formed to combat other diseases do not hesitate to play on this same emotion. The repeated emphasis that all of these fearful sicknesses may strike anyone at random triggers a wide response.

Personal experience transforms fear into a strong urge to fight back against the threat. Those who have observed members of their own family stricken by one of the dread diseases are potentially the largest donors to the search for a cure. The parents of retarded children forge a bond with others in their locality suffering the same agony and in many communities work together to establish schools and therapeutic agencies to furnish help. Franklin Roosevelt's affliction by infantile paralysis generated the March of Dimes, which financed the research that found the preventive vaccines.

Most police forces have "conscience funds" to which unapprehended malefactors may contribute anonymously and make restitution. A respectable middle-aged man, regretting a theft he committed as a youth, may send a check, sometimes a sizable one representing many times the sum he stole, to this fund. These donations are the most direct demonstration of guilt as a motive for giving, but guilt plays a more subtle role in impelling countless gifts. To hazard a guess, because proof is unavailable, the rich and the upper middle class give under this impulse more than those less fortunate. The contrast, visible to any observer, between the opportunities and comforts of rich and poor engender not only compassion but inevitably some feelings of guilt. One need only glance at the run-down schools, the sordid housing facilities, and the garbage-strewn streets of the ghetto to realize that, if the American dream had not become perverted into exalting status by amassing possessions that are neither needed nor even particularly wanted, more funds would be available for the needy.

A related but more positive impulse arises when people feel indebted to an institution which has benefited them. The press frequently carries stories of a naturalized citizen who, having prospered in this country, donates art objects, land, or money to some government institution. The newspaper story usually includes a rather inarticulate explanation, such as "I want to repay in part the debt I owe to this country for making my good fortune possible." Graduates of schools or colleges donate funds to their alma maters, feeling that they only partly paid the debt for their educations with their undergraduate tuitions. A life is saved in a hospital, and the grateful patient remembers when he is choosing recipients.

Catastrophe, striking almost anywhere in the world, loosens a flood of American gifts. News of the devastation of hurricanes, the death toll of earthquakes, or the recurring horror of famine moves a compassionate public to respond by sending money to the Red Cross or other relief agencies. Within forty-eight hours of the joint Syrian-Egyptian Yom Kippur attack of 1973 on Israel, New York's Jewish community raised $25 million in aid funds. Unlike gifts which are given annually to maintain established institutions, catastrophes attract immediate but one-time-only responses.

At the opposite end of the emotional scale from the tragedy of disaster, millions of dollars are given annually in relatively small contributions varying from $20 to $200 to worthy — and some not so worthy — causes, because techniques have been devised to make such giving enjoyable. A benefit performance for a Broadway hit attracts contributors to an organization about which the donors may know nothing, because the amount charged over and above the box office price is not much more than scalpers are receiving for a "hot ticket." The costume ball, the preview of a highly publicized movie, and the charity bazaar where rare items may be purchased — all are calculated to furnish golden sustenance to worthy causes while at the same time creating a pleasurable few hours for the donor. The fancier the names on the sponsor list of some fund-raising banquet or party, the more desirable are the invitations to pay the $100 admission ticket. If social barriers are not removed permanently, at least they are lowered sufficiently for these events so that the not-so-well-born can mingle with "society's" leaders during one cocktail hour or for an evening.

Ask a dozen Americans, particularly in the upper income groups, why they believe philanthropic giving is so widespread, and the majority will unhesitatingly reply, "Taxes." Professional fund raisers always emphasize the tax advantages to the donor that are written into the Internal Revenue Code. The tax laws provide that gifts, particularly large gifts by rich people, cost the donor only a fraction of their face values. Indeed, there are special circumstances where gifts actually result in enriching the donor.[6] Some authorities contend that philanthropy on any major organized scale would not continue to exist in America without the encouragement of these tax laws. This contention or its rebuttal are unprovable. Certainly, when a congressional committee opens hearings about tampering with these deductions, witnesses from philanthropic institutions flock to Washington to testify that their very existence is threatened. Nonetheless, before there were any income tax laws, there were major philanthropic gifts, and philanthropy, if it did not flourish on the present scale, at least existed. The huge donations by Rockefeller and Carnegie led the pack, but Leland Stanford, George Baker, and scores of others made major grants to institutions of learning long before the tax laws lent their present encouragement. Even today, non-tax-exempt philanthropic agencies such as the National Association for the Advancement of Colored People, the American Civil Liberties Union, the League of Women Voters, and certain conservation agencies that promote laws to lessen various kinds of pollution raise millions of dollars to support their programs. Also, it is well known that donors, particularly large donors, do not take advantage of the full 30 percent allowance contained in the code. In fact, on the average even major donors give less than half as much as they are encouraged to do by the code.

Probably the type of gift in which tax considerations loom largest is the creation of a major foundation. Not only do the income and inheritance taxes affect the establishment of these repositories, but Congress has passed laws regulating their conduct. Unlike the individual decision to give for a specific purpose or to aid a particular institution, the creator of a foundation intends a number of grants, spread over years, to a variety of purposes often loosely described in the foundation's charter. Because of the activities of a number of less significant foundations that were little more than instruments for financial manipulation, Congress passed mildly restrictive legislation that somewhat lessened the desirability of creating these bodies. While self-serving motives unquestionably play a part in this particular type of gift, the balanced view of a foundation executive is probably correct.

> Only the gullible will adopt the positions at either extreme, that the motive for establishing a foundation is either pure, unsullied benevolence, calling for unqualified approbation, or unrelieved venality, calling for complete condemnation. To the extent to which evidence of motivation is available in the life stories of donors and the histories of foundations, the self-denying and self-asserting reasons are mixed in ways that reflect accurately the ambivalent human condition of all of us.[7]

Posthumous gifts, comprising about 10 percent of American philanthropy annually,[8] have never received quite the approbation from society which greets munificence by the living. Francis Bacon set forth the tone with "he that defers his charity until he is dead is, if a man weighs it rightly, rather liberal of another man's than of his own."[9] The seventeenth-century Quaker prayer makes a similar point: "I expect to pass through this world but once. Any good therefore I can do, or any kindness I can show to my fellow creatures, let me do it now. Let me not defer or neglect it, for I shall not pass this way again."

One logical reason why posthumous giving is viewed as less praiseworthy arises from the many endowments granted in perpetuity to institutions that have lost their original purpose. An endowment made to Harvard in colonial times of a fund to paint the fences appreciated into the millions over two centuries, but the fences were replaced by brick walls so the fund had no use. While this is an extreme example, all too frequently the dead hand of the donor dictates waste to the living. However, it is easy to understand why men, particularly those without heirs, wish to enjoy their property throughout their lives and make their major gifts after death.

We have been examining the inner motives which prompt men to give, but almost certainly, external pressures play the most important role in the number, if not the size, of donations. Walk down the street on any of Chicago's five "Tag Days" without the protection of a tag waving from your lapel and you are fair game for the earnest volunteer solicitors dispensing them on every street corner. It is a brave pedestrian who remains immune from this appeal as others stop to purchase their tags. Quite apart from religious promptings, few can pass along the collection plate in church without adding their contribution. Even for a non-religious cause — as, for instance, when the ushers pass the clinking box at a football game to raise funds for the Olympic team or a theater audience is solicited for some cause — few pass the receptacle to the adjacent seat without dropping in a coin.

The direct telephonic appeal of a neighbor, friend, or civic leader requesting a contribution during a current fund drive exerts still greater pressure. A letter may be disregarded, although massive direct mail solicitation never fails to bring some results, but a person-to-person appeal is extremely difficult for most people to refuse. Perhaps the ultimate example of pressure to give to philanthropy has been adopted by many of New York City's most exclusive private schools. It is difficult for parents to gain admission for their children to these desirable institutions, which undoubtedly furnish superior education over all but the few best public schools in the city. Admission officers make it perfectly clear to parents seeking to enroll their children that over and above the tuition a gift is expected — nay, required — and often the exact amount is designated.

I asked a doctor, the administrator of a huge hospital complex who had proven himself an excellent fund raiser, "Why do people want to give?" His response was that no one wants to give. People give under pressure and then those who pressure them hail them for their generosity. Society puts pressures of all kinds on potential donors, penalizes those who refuse to give in a variety of ways, and praises those who submit as benefactors.

I have already indicated that I do not agree with this extreme view. The various motives of donors are interesting as a behavioral study, but the social results are more important. History demonstrates that people frequently perform good deeds for the most contemptible reasons, while others with the noblest impulses create misery. Unless we adopt the position that none of our philanthropic institutions offers any benefits whatever, we are forced to applaud the result of giving, regardless of the donor's initial motive.

CHAPTER 2

The Uneasy Marriage –
Philanthropy and Government

THE RELATIONSHIP between philanthropy and government resembles a long-enduring marriage which, like most, has had its ups and downs but continues to exist because the partners are dependent on each other. For long periods, the couple love each other and the relationship is harmonious. Then either husband (government) or wife (philanthropy) develops the fear that the other has infringed prerogatives. For a while nagging, bickering, and arguments replace the usual concord. Either concessions are made by one of the partners or, failing this, after a while the other becomes accustomed to changes in the relationship, and eventually the marriage again becomes placid.

Like most husbands, government establishes some very loose rules regulating philanthropy's conduct. Some twenty-five state legislatures have passed laws varying in their degrees of stringency, from merely requiring registration for fund solicitation all the way to demanding that agencies be licensed and regularly file financial statements. Counties, cities, towns, and even a few villages in various parts of the country have passed their own laws, which are mostly designed to prevent dishonest solicitation for unworthy causes. General examination of all of these statutes from state to village level reveals nothing that would in any way hamper a legitimate cause from soliciting funds or conducting its business.

Government's dominant role is assured by its ability to mold the tax laws to encourage or discourage contributions. If the erring wife, in the form of a philanthropic agency, oversteps governmental rules, she can be virtually cut off from major financial support by the revoking of the agency's tax-exempt status. While this severe remedy is called upon infrequently, it does occur, either when an agency is guilty of malfeasance or, more often, when an agency attempts to interfere to a prohibited degree in the governmental process by energetic efforts to influence legislation.

Government can terminate the efforts of a voluntary agency in a far more benign way. Hundreds of organizations existed in the North to assist in the fight against slavery prior to the Civil War. Obviously, their efforts ended with the Emancipation Proclamation. Of the many groups that formed to fight the abuse of child labor, only one has survived the passage of the federal legislation barring the employment of children. Women's organizations have progressed from the limited crusade for the right to vote to a more general struggle for equality.

The best historical example of how governmental action affects the focus of philanthropy occurred during the reform period of Roosevelt's New Deal, when, through such legislation as Social Security and the various welfare laws, government took over responsibility for support of the poor, which, up to that time, had been largely the province of philanthropy. As a result of the economic debacle which dragged on through the thirties, the number of rich and affluent citizens declined precipitously while the number of poor multiplied astronomically. The problem of poverty proved too intractable and involved too many citizens to leave the solution in the hands of the well-to-do and their philanthropic donations, no matter how well intentioned they might be. "The American Way" proved to be just not humane enough for America.

This pattern of government's taking over responsibility for functions previously performed by voluntary agencies recurs each time a social problem becomes too great for the limited resources of philanthropy to meet. The small community school of pioneer days, taught by a widow or housewife, gave way to the elaborate tax-supported public school system we have today. Private colleges could not expand to meet the developing demands for higher education; so the state universities and the land-grant colleges augmented the system. The search for the causes of disease, undertaken in the past by individual doctors in their own laboratories, acceded first to the more elaborate facilities established by philanthropy, such as those supported by the Rockefeller Foundation; then, when advances in scientific knowledge made modern medical research too expensive for exclusive philanthropic support, government entered the research field with a massive financial supplement through the National Institutes of Health.

As in other human affairs, opposition may be anticipated each time the status quo is disturbed. When the Social Security legislation was being debated in Congress and later in the courts, some employers insisted that their employees wear chains of paper clips around their necks as a symbolic protest against increased government participation in the protection of the needy. Every time "big government" takes on an additional task in the areas of health, housing, education, or medical care, many feel it is a defeat for the traditional American ideal of voluntarism and a blow to the efforts of private citizens to find their own remedies for the maladies of society.

On the other hand, government officials view with suspicion and hostility any moves by philanthropy which border on encroachment of established prerogatives. Perhaps the best recent instance of how philanthropy has run afoul of government was demonstrated in the stepped-up voters' registration campaigns conducted by a number of foundations and eleemosynary agencies. While these campaigns to increase enrollment were designed to be nonpartisan, southern congressmen were quick to note that the drives were uniformly conducted in poor and black precincts where historically there had been a low voter turnout. The effect of increasing the votes in these areas was to favor liberals, blacks, and opposition candidates. It is easy to understand the criticism voiced by conservatives, whites, and incumbents against this use of tax-exempt philanthropic funds.

Another potential source of discord between the usually amiable partners lies in the public education campaigns that philanthropic organizations habitually conduct as part of their fund-raising campaigns. So long as these educational efforts are limited to urging inoculation of children, or periodic health examinations, or the benefits of church attendance, government applauds. But when the effort is directed toward the desirability of more park lands, or fewer highways, or virtually any other cause that might require government action, official hackles start to rise. Government encourages philanthropy to do good — just not too much good.

Despite the partners' periodic quarrels, government gives substantial support to philanthropy in a number of ways. Certain services of a non-essential nature have become so popular that voluntary gifts have become inadequate to support enlarged activities. For example, many libraries, zoos, botanical gardens, and museums started as purely voluntary institutions. Today, though their voluntary structures remain intact, varying percentages of their revenues come from taxes, whether their source be municipal, state, or federal revenues.

Government initiates a more common form of support that occurs when officials are highly interested in furthering a program begun under voluntary auspices. A typical case would involve researchers connected with a medical school or hospital who propose a program for the isolation of a certain virus. In many such cases, government will pay not only for the entire direct costs of the research project but will allow a considerable additional sum to offset a proportional share of the institution's general administrative overhead. Not only medical experimentation, but all kinds of university-conducted scholarly research that may prove useful to the armed services, the Agriculture Department, or other bureaus may be encouraged to accept government research funds. Even such esoteric studies as the migration of birds, the conduct of dolphins, or the behavior of insect predators attract government grants. In all such situations, government controls the purse strings, but the choice of personnel, techniques, and administration is left completely in the hands of the voluntary agency.

A relatively recent development has put government in the unprecedented role of actually sponsoring as well as financing new philanthropic agencies. About 800 community action agencies were initiated and entirely financed by the Office of Economic Opportunity. Some 20 regional educational laboratories were created and sustained by the U.S. Office of Education, and the CIA has set up an unknown number of similar organizations to study political and economic conditions in foreign countries. One observer has called these agencies "quasi nongovernmental organizations" or "nonvoluntary voluntary associations." These agencies were not formed by citizens to meet community needs but were established in the voluntary pattern by government to circumvent civil service salary ranges, to attract scholars who would be unwilling to work full time for government, or to provide a freedom of innovative action denied to a government bureaucracy.[1]

By far the most common pattern for government support occurs when the responsibility for a previously voluntary program is taken over by government. A perfect case in point is the care of orphans, once a purely charitable duty. When laws were passed making the care of parentless children a government responsibility, funds to carry out the program were distributed to existing orphanages and child care agencies. These voluntary institutions changed neither their functions nor their structure, although they now receive anywhere from 70 to 100 percent of their operating revenues through taxes. In the same way, when the losses suffered by voluntary hospitals expanded beyond the capacity of philanthropy to meet them, the Medicare and Medicaid laws furnished the funds to assure continued operation. If government wished to expand its bureaucracy to the administration of orphanages and hospitals, it could easily insist, since it is assuming philanthropy's former role of meeting the losses. Up to this time, however, no such tendency has developed, and the conduct of these institutions has remained under voluntary control.

While government has not changed the structure of the individual agencies it has funded, its gradual assumption of more and more social responsibility has altered philanthropy's historic focus. As the poor, the homeless, the orphaned, the aging, and the diseased have increasingly become the responsibility of government, philanthropy has raised its sights on the economic scale to offer more and more assistance for the middle class. It is safe to predict that the trend will continue, for although government and philanthropy will remain partners, government will more and more be forced by social clamor and political demands to take full responsibility for philanthropy's former wards. As a result, philanthropy's emphasis will shift upward to such fields as religion, recreation, the arts, and private education, all of which presently receive minimal government support.

CHAPTER 3

Fund Raisers Call the Tune

DESPITE THE DIVERSE IMPULSES to give money, few gifts are made without solicitation. No one passes a pitiable figure on the street and presses a coin into his palm; however, if his hand is extended in supplication, passers-by will respond. In organized philanthropy, donors do not look for causes; they respond to appeals. These appeals vary in content all the way from a simple reminder that last year the donor gave $10 to the local Boy Scout troop to a personal visit from an elected official who outlines some pressing community need.

Fund raising is big business in America, employing thousands of people, including highly paid executives, clericals, secretaries, business machine operators, and all the other categories common to major "white collar" business. The techniques for conducting appeals and thus directing the flow of money to the tens of thousands of philanthropic agencies have been developed to a high degree of effectiveness. Book shelves can be lined with volumes on every aspect of fund raising, its history, the use of direct mail, the conduct of charity bazaars, the personal appeal, proposed programs for churches, and nearly every other nuance of solicitation.

Top-ranking fund raisers, whether they are employed by a large agency or conduct a company specializing in the field, are well compensated for their experience and skills. In a sense they are akin to industry's top sales managers, for although philanthropic endeavor is an intangible, the techniques for persuading people to part with their money resemble a high-pressure sales campaign. While interviewing a number of top fund raisers in connection with this book, I found them gifted with a sense of humor about their work and somewhat cynical in their outlook. They delighted in recounting anecdotes of manipulating the emotions of potentially large givers who ended up by being more "generous" than even informed associates thought was possible. In two books with high-sounding titles, a leading fund raiser for worthy causes recounts in detail some of his many experiences in swelling the sums that a variety of donors had initially intended to contribute.[1] The top practitioners of the profession know not only every one of the facets of human behavior outlined earlier in connection with giving (see Chapter 1), but a good many others omitted in that summary. Human frailties as well as strengths are exploited to the fullest to achieve major objectives.

Originally, the same people who conducted a "do good" program devoted part of their time to soliciting the funds which sustained it, and this is still true in smaller agencies. However, as agencies grew in size and number, the fund-raising function became separate from the planning and the programs for which the funds were raised. Larger agencies employed full-time fund raisers to supervise the solicitation, including the management of the volunteers participating in the fund appeals. Eventually, organizations developed that had no other purpose than to raise funds and disburse them to a number of autonomous member agencies. Federations of Jewish philanthropies sprang up in a number of cities where Jews represented a sizable segment of the population. Similar efforts by Catholic and Protestant laymen soon followed. The United Funds were born and their success led to United Hospital Funds' collecting for all the hospitals in the community. United College Funds formed to combine appeals. Finally, there developed professional fund-raising firms that accepted organizations as clients for charity drives.

To understand the enormous influence that fund raising has on philanthropic programming and the establishment of priorities, we must recognize that, despite advanced marketing techniques, some causes have far more appeal to donors than others. Perhaps the ideal fund-raising campaign would be for an agency which cared simultaneously for crippled children, the blind, and stray dogs. The posters and literature could then depict a heartbreaking scene of a blind man being led by a crippled child with a shivering dog attaching himself in fawning gratitude to the pathetic pair. Unluckily for fund raisers, these three categories of unfortunates already have a surplus of funds, both philanthropic and governmental, to assist them. Fund raisers are fully aware that causes which tug the heartstrings unloosen purse strings. Solicitations that

appeal mainly to the intellect — for museums, zoos, libraries, and the like — face far rougher sledding than do
hospitals, agencies dedicated to finding the cure for a disease, child care, or programs for the aged.

There are two general approaches to conducting a fund
appeal. The first and most common is to collect all the
money possible by various means for a general cause and
then tailor a program to fit within the available funds.
The health agencies, such as the Cancer Society and the
Heart Association, conduct these collections annually and
allocate the resultant funds to designated projects. If
funds are not available, a low-priority project is dropped.
The alternative approach is to set a definite sum as a
specific goal — the cost of a new college dormitory or
hospital building, say — and conduct a campaign to raise
precisely that amount. The particular drive continues
until the objective is reached and then stops. The director
of the American Alumni Council characterized these college capital fund drives as "something tangible billed as a
once-in-a-lifetime request — which, of course, they never
are."[2]

Collections of the first kind solicit as many people as can
be reached to give whatever sum they can. A successful
campaign for a specific goal proceeds on the theory that a
very few, perhaps ten, large donors contribute at least one
third of the total required, while the next one hundred
largest gifts total an equal amount. The final third of the
required sum is made up by all the rest of the donors put
together. Obviously, the collection can thrive on direct
mail solicitation, newspaper and television advertising,
and all the techniques used to appeal to a mass response.

Conversely, the campaign to raise a definite sum is virtually dependent on individual solicitation, personal and social pressures, and the rewarding of large donors with demonstrations of gratitude, such as memorial plaques or testimonial dinners.

The staff and volunteers who enlist for a campaign to raise a stated amount disperse once their objective is achieved. However, organizations that conduct annual collections are permanent, and even the volunteers re-enlist each year; therefore the collectors have a permanent stake in their fund-raising activities. It is for this reason that an efficient fund-raising organization, once built and achieving fruitful results, will continue to live should the need for the cause it sponsors decline or even disappear. It may be necessary to shift objectives: if one disease is conquered, there is always another to pose a new challenge to the victorious cohorts. The collection agency seems to be virtually immortal; at least its life span drags out as long as funds flow toward its solicitors.

As professional fund-raising firms available for hire by any agency developed, the phonies and the crooks appeared as they always do when large sums of money change hands. Some of these firms accepted assignments on a commission, taking up to 33 percent of the monies raised as a fee. Others conducted campaigns which either exaggerated the good deeds of the agency involved or simply proclaimed downright lies. As a result, some thirty legitimate firms combined in a trade association with a code of ethics that all agreed to observe. The American Association of Fund-Raising Counsel, Inc. (with headquarters in New York) agreed not to raise money for unworthy causes, or to charge on a commission basis, or to exaggerate claims, or to kick back any fees to those who influence the choice of firms. While this code is doubtless self-serving, the practices it bans emphasize the abuses common to the field.

If a legitimate firm is dubious about raising the money required by a prospective client, a study including a survey of prospective donors and an outline of a possible campaign to achieve the goal may be conducted for a fixed fee. Frequently the study discourages both fund raisers and client, which avoids an unsuccessful effort. Many of these legitimate firms specialize in particular causes. For example, one concentrates on raising money for Catholic causes, on both national and local levels. Others devote a major part of their effort to college fund drives. Still others have a majority of clients in the kindred fields of the arts and humanities. Obviously, such specialization familiarizes the fund raisers with the most likely prospects, whether these be foundations or individuals.

Unfortunately, many fund raisers are unhampered by professional ethics and are hungry for clients. A number of public relations firms and even some advertising agencies will accept fund-raising assignments when the campaign is to consist mainly of direct mail solicitation or advertisements in the various media. Anyone who responds to the vast number of small agency appeals that arrive each day in the mail would not only be naive, he would soon be bankrupt.

Some fund-raising effort is at the opposite extreme from the soft sell of the easy-to-throw-away letter or the advertisement to which no one is forced to respond. Hard-sell fund raising involves social pressures, business considerations, and community acceptance. The most virulent, and to many the most unpleasant, technique is the public announcement at a huge gathering of the size of individual gifts or pledges by those in the audience. Cards listing donors' names and their records of previous gifts are held by a master of ceremonies. As his name is read out, the donor responds; thus his peers are in a position to judge the "generosity" of the gift. This practice is used in major Jewish campaigns conducted in a number of localities. There is no doubt it is productive, for huge sums are raised. "It's awful, but it's the most effective way of raising money," said a leader of New York's Jewish community.[3] However, it is a cause of embarrassment and an invasion of privacy; fortunately the practice is not widespread.

In a very few cases, an even more extreme pressure, the threat of job loss, may be used to extort gifts. Staff doctors in one metropolitan hospital were told that their privileges to hospitalize their private patients would be revoked unless each donated a specific sum. As most doctors perform services without fee on patients unable to pay, they feel particularly outraged when, in addition, monetary contributions are demanded of them.

With the total separation of fund raising from programming, major philanthropic agencies have inevitably changed their viewpoint. Such new factors as the condition of the national economy, price levels in the various security markets, and other considerations tend to take precedence over social needs as the predominant criteria. Obviously, if money cannot be raised for a new program, the program cannot be instituted. If money continues to flow because of strong emotional appeal or because of an efficient organization, programs will endure although the necessity for them may have declined. To a large degree, it is not social planners, studying the overall needs of our society, who come up with a neat blueprint for sorely needed projects. Rather, it is trained fund raisers, conducting objective market surveys of potential gifts, who have virtual veto power over unappealing innovations and can assure longevity to agencies whose years of maximum usefulness are often behind them.

CHAPTER 4

The United Way—
Giving Without Feeling

ANYONE WHO HAS WALKED down a street in Bombay or
Calcutta crowded with beggars stretching out emaciated
hands in supplication knows the acute discomfort caused
by a multiplicity of charitable appeals. Each of the many
"do good" agencies established in the nineteenth century
sought community support for their work. A more efficient fund-raising device was required to reduce the
number of appeals, and the idea of federating agencies
into a single campaign was imported from England, where
it had been inaugurated in Liverpool in 1873. Clergymen
from that city emigrated, and by 1887 the first American
joint campaign was instituted in Denver.[1] Quite apart
from the advantage of reducing the number of appeals,
consolidation permitted the replacement of volunteers by
professional solicitors. The movement gathered support
around the turn of the century, when the Jewish communities in Cincinnati and Boston adopted it for the agencies
they sponsored. Experience in these two cities demonstrated an increase in the total amounts collected as well as

longer lists of contributors. The number of relief agencies that sprang up during World War I gave further impetus to the federation idea. A United War Fund was created with the encouragement of government officials. Just as the war ended, a huge appeal was underway and over $200 million had been raised, which was later distributed to the participating agencies. Out of the war drive grew Community Chests in virtually every moderate-sized or large community, and during the 1920s these organizations multiplied tenfold.

During World War II, the Community Chests raised funds beyond anything then believed possible, because business, labor, and the public responded to patriotic appeals. After the war, donations declined although individual agencies' needs rose; again, a multitude of individual fund appeals threatened the federated concept. After 1947, at the instigation of Henry Ford in Detroit, the United Funds were instituted, largely to put a stop to the multiplication of in-plant solicitations, which reduced the efficiency of cooperating companies. Employers, gratified by the prospect of only one annual solicitation on company property, enthusiastically cooperated.

Today, under its changed title, the United Way conducts campaigns in nearly 2200 American communities; in 1973 it raised a total of over $900 million. Employees gave 61.7 percent; corporate gifts totaled 28.9 percent; and the remainder came from foundations and the public at large. Allocations from this huge total were: 28 percent to family and child care agencies; a whopping 27 percent for such recreational services as the Boy Scouts and the Camp Fire Girls; 13 percent to the Red Cross; 10 percent to other health services; and 16 percent for administration and fund raising.[2]

Criticism of federated solicitation arose almost from the beginning of the movement, and while the tone has changed somewhat over the years, the faultfinding continues to this day. The wide support of the business community had sprung originally from the belief and hope that the number of campaigns would be greatly reduced. At first there was even a prospect of eliminating all other appeals so that a community could put "all its begs in one ask it." This hope proved illusory because agencies not participating in the Chest drives declined to cease their own fund-raising activities, which would have been tantamount to committing agency suicide. Inclusion in a Chest drive became more an official seal of approval than an all-embracing program. It is doubtful that the current United Way has decreased the number of appeals, although it has consolidated the larger and less controversial local agencies into one solicitation. It has further achieved one of the prime goals of its supporters: reduction of in-plant solicitation to the one official fund-raising drive sponsored by business.

The corporate sponsorship of United Funds, which assures the success of these drives, also stirs some of the most bitter criticism. Employee resentment is typified by such comments as "They sure twist your arm around here to give to the damned United Fund," and "We want to give to the best of our ability, not be victimized by our supervisors . . . [They] use scare tactics to squeeze out what has been arbitrarily designated as our fair share."[3]

Quite apart from donor dissatisfaction, critics of United

Funds contend that business sponsorship and the participation in decision-making by corporate executives pro-
duces a conservative and non-responsive attitude to
developing social needs. Whitney Young, the late spokes-
man for the Urban League, pointed out that of the $440
million collected by United Funds in the ninety-seven
cities where the League operates, only 1.5 percent of the
total raised went into programs run by and for blacks,
Puerto Ricans, and Mexican Americans.[4] A black leader
in San Francisco, Tom Gwyn, said bitterly, "Their [the
United Funds'] idea of solving social problems is to give
sailing lessons to the Camp Fire Girls."[5] Blacks have at-
tacked the Funds in Cleveland and in other cities. In
Boston, one black organization pulled out of the Fund.
In Philadelphia, when black pressures forced an allocation in support of legal services for the poor, the city's
police reduced their contributions by 65 percent. As a result, the Philadelphia Fund failed to reach its goal for the
first time in years. The director's comment was, "The best
climate for a United Fund Campaign is a calm sea — when
you don't have people taking issue."[6]

Critics further contend that once an agency is added to
the Funds' roster, the people previously interested in
raising funds for it lose much of their enthusiasm and
energy. Moreover, supporters feel that they no longer
have direct responsibility for the agency's success or failure. When a campaign concludes, there is apt to be bitter-
ness on the part of individual agencies, particularly those
that have recently joined, over the small share of the total
allocated to them. One authority stated, "Community
Chest Drives came about not by willing cooperation

among the fund-raising organizations, but rather in response to the pressure of enraged citizens who were just
tired of being besieged by so many fund raisers."[7]

The basic reason for much of the criticism leveled at
United Funds is that their primary purpose is to raise
money, not to assess periodically the priorities of programs
for social improvement. However, as we have seen, the
most needed services, those which the public most willingly supports and thus those with the greatest fund-
raising appeal, are the first to receive partial or total
government support. For the past several years, most hospitals have no longer required philanthropic subsidy to
balance their operating budgets; nevertheless, local
United Funds continue listing community hospitals on
their roster of beneficiary agencies. As one suburban
United Fund executive told me, failure to list hospitals
would hamper fund raising for the other agencies, because
donors place the highest priority on giving for health and
medical causes. The mere fact that the need has lessened
does not inhibit the enthusiastic fund raisers from pro-
ceeding exactly as in the past. All federated drives which
have traditionally included hospitals as component parts
face the same dilemma. The Federation of Jewish Philanthropies of New York, for example, continues to list its
affiliated hospitals as a major reason for its appeal. I once
suggested to a horror-stricken Federation executive that
hospitals should discontinue their affiliation except for
occasional major capital fund drives. "That would be the
end of Federation," he told me. "Without the hospitals
our appeals would lose their emotional impact." In a full-
page advertisement in the *New York Times* inaugurating

a recent campaign of the United Fund of Greater New York, hospitals headed the list of institutions that were to be beneficiaries, although their needs for philanthropic funds were less than those of any other category. In short, the United Funds need the hospitals even if the hospitals don't need the United Funds.

Just as fund-raising considerations oppose dropping agencies with proven appeal, so countervailing pressures create inertia in establishing new programs, however badly needed, if they lack such appeal. The emergence of new social needs creates novel and often difficult problems for the fund raiser; the status quo assumes all the attractions of the non-controversial, the tried and tested. While no United Fund executives would publicly espouse the sentiment, the truth is that their functions would be rendered relatively painless if each year the same agencies were beneficiaries and the slightly increased budgets and goals were merely established to offset the creeping inflation which donors now understand. But when an old agency has to be dropped because its functions have been taken over by government or its program has become obsolete, controversy arises over the exclusion. In the same way, the addition of a new agency to the list of beneficiaries introduces the controversial questions: "Who needs it?" and "Why should we enter this field?"

While the United Way dwarfs all other federated fund drives, it is by no means the sole example of a multiple-agency appeal. In all major cities, each of the three leading religious groups mounts an annual drive to sustain the health and welfare agencies they sponsor, and the nation-wide totals add up to an imposing amount. The financially pressed black colleges of the South consolidated their individual appeals into the United Negro College Fund. In several communities where interest in cultural activities has expanded, councils for the arts have been established to distribute jointly raised money to the various museums, symphonies, and civic operas of the area. During the Vietnam war, a number of peace organizations joined in a single drive.

Our conclusion must be that consolidated fund raising and particularly the United Way, despite all the criticism it merits, is useful and convenient for all concerned. The donor feels that with one gift he has fulfilled his philanthropic obligations. The established agencies are assured of continuing support. Cooperating employers benefit by agreeing to only one fund drive a year. Indeed, it would be difficult to suggest an alternative. The United Funds themselves realize that better justification will be required in the future for their fund-raising efforts and their methods of allocation. The point is made clear in a 1969 study by the United Community Funds and Councils of America entitled "Projections for the Seventies." This handsome and carefully researched pamphlet attempts to predict the direction of philanthropy in the decade ahead. The report urges United Fund executives to gird themselves for the struggle to keep pace with the future. "United Funds must develop a case for support which documents locally why United Fund growth must keep pace with or exceed economic growth. In the absence of a convincing case, givers may well draw the conclusion that as the economy expands, voluntary health and welfare services should contract."[8]

The truth is that far more is required than the type of justification called for in this summation. If we examine the roster of agencies supported by our local United Funds, we will find little change in the listings over the past decade or even the last twenty years. Some harsh questions should be asked. Is it really in the best interests of our society to allocate over 27 percent of the $900 million total to the Boy Scouts and kindred recreational services? Is it not high time to reassess the United Funds' allocations to the various voluntary health agencies in view of the far greater sums appropriated by government for the same causes? Should not hospitals be dropped from the roster, despite their fund-raising appeal, in view of the trifling United Fund contribution to the massive financial outlays of these modern institutions? These and many similar questions should be asked, but I have no hope that they will be or that they would evoke answers. The United Way will continue on its safely worthy course, supporting well-established agencies, avoiding controversy, and with the conservative eyes of its policy makers firmly fixed on yesterday's needs.

CHAPTER 5

Trustees—The Abdication
of Responsibility

IN THE FALTERING FORWARD STEPS that men have taken to develop methods of governing themselves and their institutions, a wide gap has existed between theory and reality. The theorists who design systems of governance contemplate that rulers will be virtuous men, committed to their duties, informed on the issues, judicial in their decisions, motivated by the public welfare and not private interest. The authors of the American Constitution did not envisage rigged elections' stilling the voices of thousands of citizens who on one pretext or another are disenfranchised. Nor did they foresee the development of such political machines as Tammany Hall in its heyday or mayors of the ilk of Boston's James Curley or Chicago's Richard Daley. Nor did Russians theorizing about their government after their revolution foresee an autocracy as centralized as the one they had known under the czars. In theory, the policies of American corporations are dictated by the owners, the stockholders, who vote in democratic fashion for their representatives on boards of directors. Reality distorts this image until it is almost unrecognizable. In much the same way, our present system of governance for voluntary institutions, developed through logic and dictated by economics and the experience of the past, has lost much of its relevance and effectiveness in providing leadership for the present.

Historically, the criteria for membership on boards of trustees were based on economic logic. When a community discovered a social need and organized to take remedial steps, those able and willing to furnish the funds necessary to accomplish the purpose were the obvious candidates for leadership through membership on the governing body. Thus, around a century ago, the founders of what are today America's great voluntary hospitals established institutions that were to serve them in time of illness and, incidentally, to serve the poor as well. Opera companies, orchestras, and art museums were similarly established by rich music lovers and art fanciers. Having indicated their commitment with their checkbooks, these people were the logical ones to decide how the money they donated or solicited from others was to be spent.

Keeping pace with this developing pattern, the various states promulgated laws permitting the incorporation of these institutions on a non-profit basis and holding the trustees on the governing boards responsible for the conduct of their agencies. Originally, the trustees received no compensation for time devoted to the institution—a practice which continues almost universally to this day. Indeed, as the board members were responsible for raising the money to meet deficits, it would have been absurd for them to shift money from one pocket into another to pay themselves. As increasing social needs forced these institutions to expand, it became impossible for trustees to handle the day-to-day administration of their agencies. Therefore, the professional, whether educator, doctor, curator, or social worker, entered the organizational structure of college, hospital, museum, or welfare agency as the paid administrator, employed by the trustees to conduct routine duties. His degree of power to hire and fire his staff varies in different agencies according to the latitude granted by the boards. In some, the administrator can hardly buy a gross of paper clips without board approval. In others, the widest latitude is accorded within the framework of an approved budget. But despite differences in practice, the structure of board of trustees, administrator, and professional staff is today's pattern.

Just as history explains the development of the basic system of governance common to nearly all philanthropic institutions, evolutionary trends hold the key to the current shift in power away from trustees toward administrators and professional staff. When we previously discussed the relationship between government and philanthropy, we observed that government moved primarily into those erstwhile philanthropic areas representing the most urgent social needs. Thus today public funding has virtually replaced philanthropic donation in major voluntary hospitals, child care agencies, most libraries, and, to a lesser degree, educational institutions. As government support and consumer payments replaced the major donations of trustees of these institutions, the professional administrator widened his authority over both the executive and the policy-making function. No longer having to solicit trustees to meet financial deficits, he ceased to feel he required their approval for expenditures. And the trustees, grateful for the cessation of never-ending requests for money, were only too glad to devote more attention to their business activities, their law practices, or whatever careers occupied the major portion of their time. Over the years, institutions — whether hospitals, universities, or social work agencies — grew in size and complexity, and scientific advances rendered the layman's knowledge much more inadequate. As a result, the professional administrator found board consultation increasingly time-consuming, onerous, and unhelpful. At the same time, lack of detailed knowledge of the growing institution's complex problems caused board members to feel ill-equipped to proffer the advice that had been graciously received in the past. In short, for many reasons the administrator welcomed wider powers at the precise time when board members were willing to surrender active responsibility.

I can illustrate this transition from my own experience. When World War II ended, the antibiotic miracle drugs that had been developed as part of wartime research became available for general use but at a prohibitively high cost because mass production had not begun. As a trustee of a major voluntary hospital, I joined in the board room deliberations about making these expensive new drugs available to ward patients who obviously had no means to pay for their lifesaving administration. One quarter of the hospital's annual budget of $4 million came from philanthropy, with the remainder flowing from Blue Cross payments, the patients themselves, and the municipality, which furnished partial payment for the indigent. Obviously, the debate was not over the desirability of furnishing these drugs to poor patients but only over how to meet the huge new costs. It was finally decided to instruct the medical staff to use these drugs whenever patient welfare dictated, and the Board pledged somehow to raise the additional funds. Here was a policy decision involving medical practice — and, indeed, the very lives of patients entering the institution. Today, when hospital incomes are supplemented by government to the point where philanthropy has virtually no responsibility to meet deficits, a debate at this level would be unthinkable.

This evolution has been aptly summarized, in a study by Herman and Anne Somers:

> Ultimate responsibility for policy has always rested with lay trustees. In the past, this usually meant fund raising and — all too frequently — making up operating deficits out of their own pockets. In recent years, however, the tremendous rise in hospital costs, the increasing role of government in capital funding, the decreased likelihood that hospitals will end the year in the red, the growing size and complexity of hospital operations, and the growing professionalization of hospital administration have all tended to down-grade the trustee vis-à-vis the administrator. While the trustee's legal responsibility has not diminished, his role and status have.[1]

In institutions still dependent on philanthropic funds for their survival, the responsibility and role of the trustees more nearly resembles the original theory. While hospitals, public libraries, and the most important voluntary child care agencies receive sufficient government funding to assure continuity, museums, private schools and colleges, group work agencies, the performing arts, and the various recreational and camp endeavors do not. Power flows from the purse, and because the trustees maintain control of it, the administrator and his staff do not have the same latitude of action as when finances are assured. Nonetheless, as professionalism has developed in education, social work, and the arts, trustees are increasingly dependent upon staff for the data on which to base their decisions. Obviously, the way the data are assembled and presented affects the final policy decision. In institutions blessed with large or even adequate endowments, the administrator tends to have wider latitude than in situations in which each new expenditure adds to a deficit that must be covered by raising additional funds.

We are most apt to observe the trustee in his classic role of being truly responsible in those philanthropic agencies primarily devoted to fund raising. In United Funds, civic federations of philanthropies, and the various health agencies which raise funds in order to distribute them to research or patient care, trustees take a more active role — at least in the solicitation aspects of the agencies' activities. Distributions of the funds is likely to be routine, granting those agencies which received funds in the previous year a renewal allocation of the same or a slightly larger size. However, trustees do have to make policy decisions when funds are to flow in a new direction or, more rarely, when they are to be withheld from agencies that have become obsolete. A representative of each supported agency customarily also sits as a trustee of most united and federated funds. These representatives act as ambassadors, to assure that their agencies receive their just share of the total, but it is unusual for agency representatives to sit on the all-important distribution committee, which decides the allocations.

Three distinct types of boards have developed. The first is the purely fund-raising board of the type that presides over local United Funds and other federated campaigns. These boards are concerned with such activities as advertising, enlisting volunteers, public relations, public education, and organized solicitation. They have little or nothing to do with the programs of the institutions for which the money is raised. In contrast, the boards of the constituent agencies, which have agreed to merge their fund raising into a joint effort, are untroubled by the mundane routines of raising money and presumably address themselves to fulfilling the social program their agency has embraced, be it child adoption, care of unwed mothers, disaster relief, or day care of children. These agencies require minimal trustee participation, because the professional social worker, doctor, or librarian in administrative charge is far more highly trained in program development than are the lay board members. The third type of board follows the historic pattern whereby members have the joint responsibility for raising deficit funds and thus remain in control of programming. These boards are limited to institutions which neither are part of a joint fund-raising effort nor receive substantial government subsidy. Examples are found in fine arts museums; operas, symphonies, and other performing companies; smaller social work agencies excluded from United Funds; and non-tax-exempt organizations.

When voluntary institutions become unresponsive to

public needs or to the particular demands of their con-
stituencies, the first point of attack is the governing body.
Action pictures of rioting students on college campuses
cause the public to ask indignantly, "Who's in charge
here?" Picket lines around besieged urban hospitals do
not always mean a labor dispute is in progress; sometimes
community groups mount these demonstrations to demand
health services presently denied. Angry artists protesting
either the political orientation or the irrelevance of some
museum exhibition demand an audience with the trustees.
Not only are these institutions subjected at present to
outside criticism for the way they are conducted, but a
period of the most rigorous self-examination is underway.
Colleges are establishing committees including alumni,
faculty, and students to study the flaws in present governing structures and to recommend reform. Trustees of
medical facilities are keenly aware of the growing demands for "community control" and are debating their
response. Trustees of other institutions, aware of the
mounting criticism, are asking themselves who they really
represent and whether they are in fact anything but
honorary rubber stamps for virtually autonomous administrators.

Particularly articulate criticism, as would be expected,
comes from the academic community. Here is Morton
Rauh of Antioch College:

> Unfortunately, management by trustees no longer has mean-
> ing. The gap between the stated responsibilities of trustees
> and their capacity to execute them is starkly demon-
> strated in the section of the Ohio General Code that defines
> the duties of Ohio State University trustees, which says that

they "shall fix and regulate the course of instruction and pre-
scribe the extent and character of experiments to be made at
the University."

While such nonsense offers no guidance for what Ohio
State's trustees should do, it may sorely tempt them into doing
what they should not do.

All over the country trustees are playing games. They act
as if they *decide* issues, which, in fact, they cannot possibly
do.[2]

Or take another scholar, John Kenneth Galbraith, address-
ing himself to the same problem:

> The governing structure of the older and more mature Ameri-
> can universities is almost certainly obsolete. Specifically,
> what should have been a transitional arrangement for a
> particular stage of development has been allowed to become
> permanent. In the last century a governing board of business-
> men, bankers, and lawyers (along with churchmen), selected
> for their respectability and general eminence in the world of
> affairs, made a measure of sense . . . [Today] a lay board
> can, by its nature, have little comprehension of the vast and
> complex scientific and scholarly life of the university it
> presumes to govern.[3]

In the rising chorus of criticism, the first charge leveled
against institutional trustees — and one that can hardly be
refuted — is that they are essentially undemocratic, self-
perpetuating, and unrepresentative of either the community or even the institutional clients. The common process
of selecting trustees supports the charges. Usually a nominating committee of the existing board recommends
additions or replacements for membership, and because
the nominations are bound to be made from among lists of
friends or acquaintances, these boards more nearly re-

semble clubs than policy-making congresses. Aging board members who find their time and energies limiting the frequency of their attendance at meetings sometimes offer their resignations on the condition that one of their children replace them. Thus, it is not uncommon for trusteeships to assume the same hereditary characteristics as fortunes, real estate, or business enterprises. This practice is so widely established that it is described by a chairman of a nominating committee with some pride:

> I recently went to our hospital treasurer who was one of the older trustees and made this suggestion to him: "Why not retire and put your son on the board?" The son is 45, an attorney and a good one. "You are spending your winters in Florida and your summers playing golf," I pointed out. "What more are you going to contribute?"
>
> He was good enough to take my suggestion. I repeated the performance with another board member. I even prepared a replacement for myself by enlisting my son-in-law . . .[4]

When we examine the composition of boards selected in this conventional manner, we discover the proof that the criticism is well founded. Consider, for example, the findings of a commission established to study the governance of Yale:

> The [10] successor trustees who perpetuate themselves by electing their own replacements — and, even more so, the [9] trustees elected by the alumni — have been drawn overwhelmingly from a narrow stratum of society. Women, blacks, Jews, Catholics, and other persons, however distinguished, who are not members of the more favored groups in society have only recently begun to take seats.[5]

In a wide sampling of the backgrounds of both the trustees of the Los Angeles Community Chest and its many constituent agencies, conducted between 1962 and 1965, a researcher concluded the following. In the first place, the trustees were not young; 69 percent of those interviewed were in the fifty-to-seventy-year age group. Males outnumbered females two to one; 87 percent were married and four fifths of these had children. These leaders were predominantly Republican (67 percent); 98 percent were Caucasians. As to economic class, only 5 percent earned under $10,000 a year, while 15 percent had incomes between $50,000 and $100,000 a year. Between these extremes, the remaining trustees were divided thus: 32 percent between $10,000 and $19,000; 18 percent between $20,000 and $29,000; 10 percent between $30,000 and $39,000; and 8 percent between $40,000 and $49,000. Half were college graduates and 57 percent were in professions which could be classified as business, finance, or management.[6]

A study of the biographical data on the trustees of some 500 public and private schools conducted in 1968 disclosed that the typical college trustee was male, white, Protestant, in his fifties, a politically moderate Republican; more than half of the 5000 trustees who responded to this poll earned at least $30,000 a year. The majority believed that faculties should have little power in decision-making and students still less.[7] Another study in 1969 disclosed that only 5 percent of college trustees were under forty, although at that time anyone over twenty-five was in the older half of the population. In addition, while 80 percent of American families then had annual incomes of less than $10,000, only 8 percent of the trustees studied were earning that little.[8]

No perfect number of members exists for the ideal board of trustees. Harvard's Corporation, its board of trustees under another name, has only 7 members. Certainly such a closely knit group should have less difficulty in reaching decisions than, say, the 37 trustees of New York's Museum of Modern Art. Perhaps an extreme example of unwieldy size is the American Cancer Society with its Board of 114 members, half of whom are physicians or dentists and half laymen. This Board met three times in 1972 with an average attendance of 80 members. The Executive Committee consisted of 25 Board members, certainly a more efficient size, but this group met only once in the same year, with 23 present. The American Heart Association Board numbers about 120; the American Lung Association, 121. Both groups customarily meet twice a year. By New York State law, boards of trustees of county libraries may not comprise fewer than 5 members or more than 11. The major factor leading to large boards is that they have no personnel turnover except that caused by death or resignation. Many institutions elect trustees for a specified term, usually three years, but in virtually all cases, once elected they are re-elected term after term. Unless bylaws prevent re-election, the member dropped from a board of trustees is bound to feel resentment since he has served conscientiously and in most cases has donated at least some money to the cause. As there is no particular reason to antagonize a hitherto loyal supporter, it is easier to keep all persons on the roster whether their attendance at meetings or their continuing support of the agency warrants it. As a result, the deadwood grows: it is not unusual for a board to consist of a majority of inactive members.

The executive committee empowered to act for the board between meetings evolves as a true substitute body by reason of its more efficient size, and its members' greater interest and more regular attendance.

The National Information Bureau, a generally excellent agency which evaluates the work of philanthropic institutions in many fields, has established standards for awarding its stamp of approval. Heading these standards is: "#1 — BOARD — An active and responsible governing body, serving without compensation, holding regular meetings and with effective administrative control." Contained in this statement is every one of the misleading clichés that prevents close examination and reform of the trustee structure. "Governing body" is used; not "policy-formulating body." Coupled with governing is "administrative control," which clearly should not and almost never lies in the hands of the board. Here is an agency which judges other agencies, and on this one point it is just as fuzzy in articulating its criteria as are the agencies it judges.

The laws of the various states support the bylaws of the philanthropic institutions by outlining again in the traditional terms the overall responsibility of the trustees. But at least in some states — New York is one — the pertinent membership corporation law relieves trustees of personal liability for events transpiring in their institutions. The New York law reads: "In the absence of fraud or bad faith the directors of a membership corporation . . . shall not be personally liable for its debts, obligations or liabilities." Obviously, the purpose of the law was to make it more attractive for uncompensated trustees to accept appointment, as they might be very loath to do if liability accompanied responsibility.

Thoughtful people agree that the trustee system badly needs reform and a redefinition of role, but no consensus exists as to the nature of this reform. To make boards more democratic, universities and other philanthropic institutions have in recent years added to their trustees more women, some blacks, and a few younger people. Militants and liberals have campaigned for "community control" of local institutions, but where such duly elected bodies have been tried, as in New York City's public schools, chaos has resulted. The fact is that operating institutions, like ships and corporations, cannot prosper under democratic control.

Nevertheless, philanthropy should establish some mechanism for receiving community input. A middle ground must be found between the present method of choosing trustees who are completely non-representative of agency clients and the other extreme of so much client domination that anarchy results. One orderly method of experimenting with reform would be to limit the period of trusteeship to three to five years. By adding more representative new trustees, present boards would maintain control by majority vote, but at least they would be exposed to varying viewpoints during policy debate.

Under the present system, the only important function that most boards still retain is the selection of the professional administrator, whose advice is docilely followed during his tenure of office. On the level of our national government, the uneasy feeling persists that the executive's growing power has usurped the authority of Congress, but little to remedy the situation has been suggested. A similar situation has evolved in the governance of our voluntary agencies, and a restoration of more balanced power is urgently required.

CHAPTER 6

The Overstressed Foundations

WHEN A RESEARCHER informs people that he is engaged in a study of philanthropy, most will nod wisely and say, "Oh, yes, a book about foundations." Certainly the flow of articles and books regarding foundation activities is massive. Some are muckraking exposés based largely on congressional committee transcripts of testimony in connection with tax reform. Other studies are scholarly reviews of the history and activities of the largest foundations. As a result of these many publications, uninformed people draw the conclusion that foundation grants set the trends for philanthropic giving and even represent the bulk of total contributions.

Perhaps the explanation for this widespread equating of one small facet of the subject with the whole lies in history, for it is certainly true that the early foundations — Rockefeller, Carnegie, Russell Sage, Twentieth Century Fund, and others — did have a tremendous impact on the direction of American philanthropy in the early decades of the century. A number of less logical reasons explains why a minor segment is identified with the aggregate. For one thing, donations by at least the major foundations are open to public scrutiny, and the largest grants receive wide publicity. Even the activities of lesser foundations can be studied by any diligent researcher without inconvenience, because nearly all available data are assembled in one location — The Foundation Center Library in New York City.

Another reason for the exaggeration of the impact of foundations originates with the fund raisers for those worthy causes that might be eligible for grants. These pleaders, their palms outstretched, are well aware that foundation money has already been given; indeed, the sole function of foundations is to distribute already donated funds. Thus a supplicant only has to argue that his cause deserves support. Unlike the individual donor, who must first be convinced to part with his money, foundations are forced by law to distribute theirs. Because of this pressure to distribute, the foundations, at least the larger ones, are not frightened by the magnitude of institutional requests for largess; in many cases, applications for large sums for major projects are more welcome than requests for smaller amounts required by more modest endeavors.

Yet another factor that contributes to the inflated image of foundation influence is that paid staff members of the larger ones have the job of publicizing their employers' good works as well as investigating the merits of requests. These professional distributors of wealth, constituting a small, elite body, are not likely to underemphasize their importance either to the public or, more particularly, to hopeful applicants. They have given themselves the generic title of "philanthropoids," and virtually no conference on education, social work, or any other philanthropic area can be held in the United States without the presence of representative philanthropoids. Because they are knowledgeable and make it their professional duty to be experts in many facets of the field, they frequently contribute more to the discussion and leadership at these conferences than either their numbers or the money they can contribute represents. Needless to say, few representatives of the fund-seeking institutions at the conference, whether they be college presidents, hospital executives, or social work administrators, are apt to cut short the expression of views by a philanthropoid. Mental or even written notes may be taken as to how to reframe applications for grants in order to conform to a philanthropoid's expressed views. Rarely do individual donors, busy about their own tasks, attend such conferences, even though the available money that a few of them, if they united, could give would far surpass the foundation grants. Even when an individual benefactor does attend, he is apt to remain silent in the presence of the flow of professional expertise.

The Foundation Center estimates that there exist 25,000 to 30,000 foundations in the United States. This estimate includes private, community, corporate-financed, and family foundations. Before the fall of security values, their combined wealth totaled approximately $30 billion, and in 1973 they made grants of about $2.4 billion. This amount, while imposing, was less than 10 percent of the total given or bequeathed to all philanthropy in that year. Some four fifths of the foundations had assets of less than $500,000 and made grants of less than $25,000 during the year. These were instrumentalities designed either to lessen tax burdens or to act as interim recipients for funds awaiting final distribution. At the other end of the scale, 34 foundations each had assets of over $100 million (see Appendix A, p. 171).[1]

In recent years, committees of the Congress and the Internal Revenue Service have taken jaundiced looks at the financial activities of foundations in general and of a number of specific family foundations in particular. Anyone who reads the verbatim transcripts of subcommittee hearings on this subject will find dozens of citations of tax dodging, of establishing foundations better to control family-owned businesses, and even more damaging evidence of conflict of interest, self-enrichment, and downright dishonesty. These disclosures make lively reading and Joseph C. Goulden in his book *The Money Givers* makes the best of his opportunity.[2] In late 1969 Congress passed some mildly remedial legislation designed to curb the worst abuses, but there is no doubt that close and critical official scrutiny of the foundations continues.

The subject of my study, however, is not financial manipulation or chicanery by donors but rather the effect of foundation giving on the country's philanthropic structure. A thesis with some such title as "Doing Bad by Doing Good" could be advanced in criticism of some large foundation activity. As an example, the Ford Foundation's encouragement of decentralization in the governing structure of New York City's public school system was conceived as an idealistic response to one of the community's toughest problems. For years the education of the city's black children had been unacceptably inferior. A committee appointed by the Mayor, including the President of the Ford Foundation, recommended an experiment in three locations in which local community control would be substituted for the existing centralized supervision of the Board of Education. The Foundation granted $163,000 to institute the plan.[3] The new community boards had scarcely taken their seats when they began to insist on personnel changes that brought on a conflict with the teachers' union. A strike of the whole school system followed. Nasty racial tensions were fanned between the predominantly Jewish membership of the union and the blacks who supported the local boards. The conflict was eventually settled by compromise legislation passed in Albany and acceptable to the union. However, the whole episode raised the serious question of how far private foundations should interfere with public institutions. The education of New York City's black children is still a disgrace, and there is continuing disagreement as to whether any improvement has occurred as a result of the modified decentralization.[4]

The publicity attendant on large foundation grants sometimes heightens expectations, which later turn to disillusionment when programs begun with high hopes fail to achieve goals. This often occurs when a foundation awards a matching grant that is difficult if not impossible to meet. Attended by considerable fanfare, the Ford Foundation bestowed $80 million on hard-pressed symphony orchestras in many American cities. The grant stretched over the years, and each community was required to raise an equal sum from its music lovers. Symphonies sprang to life with high hopes, but many cities that had met trouble supporting their orchestras in the past found it impossible to raise the matching funds. Aspirations flickered and died, and many symphonies returned to their moribund status.

A number of major corporations have established foundations as conduits for their philanthropic donations. The tax laws encourage corporate gifts by allowing up to 5 percent of profits to be deducted if contributed to tax-exempt institutions. But far from approaching this figure, total corporate giving in 1973 was less than 1 percent of total profits: according to estimates, $950 million was given, whereas total profits were $126 billion.[5] It is not difficult to understand that corporate managers, anxious to satisfy stockholders by declaring larger dividends, are reluctant to make heavy inroads into their profits by giving them away. While corporate foundations are a common instrument for major companies, many corporations choose to make their contributions directly to the recipients. In the discussion that follows, no distinction is made between these two approaches.

Obviously, corporate management wishes to avoid public controversy over gifts made out of profits. The most non-controversial recipients are the local United Funds; so 30 percent of all corporate gifts flow to them. Engineering schools such as MIT and universities offering business education such as the University of Pennsylvania's Wharton School and Harvard's business school are favored for the obvious reason that large companies constantly require young graduates with the training to be tomorrow's leaders. More recently, some major companies have lent assistance to encourage the arts. Mobil, Exxon,

Bristol-Myers, and others have contributed funds to educational television stations for the presentation of superior films.[6] Several companies, including RCA, Reader's Digest, Prudential Life Insurance, Bristol-Myers, and Corning Glass, joined together in 1974 to form the National Corporate Fund for Dance, with a proposed first-year budget of $300,000.[7] Though this total is modest, the multicompany approach to a single art form constitutes something of an innovation in corporate giving.

While it is safe to generalize that corporate philanthropy is rarely innovative, there have been notable exceptions. The foundation established by U.S. Steel has supported some exploration efforts in Antarctica and research in nutrition and preventive medicine. No critic could contend that such projects were directly connected with the public relations of a major steel producer.

Despite the imposing billion-dollar total of corporate gifts, the fact remains that the percentage of profits allocated to philanthropy has declined from a high of over 1 percent in 1964 to 0.75 percent in 1973.[8] With the current squeeze on profits, it is safe to predict that the dollar total will decline in the immediate future. The large private foundations are also affected by corporate profits and fluctuations in security prices. In the fall of 1974, the Ford Foundation announced that its assets had declined from $3 billion to $2 billion and disclosed that it was considering a reduction of its annual grants by as much as 50 percent. Carnegie Foundation soon followed, with an announcement that its assets had dropped from $336 million to $210 million and that grants in the next year would be cut by $500,000.[9]

Whether dictated by the harsh realities of the market-place or the priority of needs, foundation decision-making is based more on intellect and less on emotion than is giving by individuals. Therefore the proportions flowing to the different aspects of philanthropy diverge from the total of all giving. For example, religion's 43 percent share of the total is twenty times the proportion that the foundations grant to this category. On the other hand, the foundations grant 36 percent to education as opposed to 16 percent given from all sources. The humanities also receive a greater percentage of aid from the foundations than they do from the public as a whole. However, it must be re-emphasized that the dollar aid to any of these areas given by the foundations is only a small part of all gifts.

Spokesmen for foundations stress the function of their "seed money," or their innovative role, as the principle reason why these institutions are of value to society. They point with pride to past achievements, such as the Rocke-feller-financed Flexner Report with its profound impact on the delivery of health care. They cite as well Rockefeller's early support to Dr. Jonas Salk's research on polio and the Guggenheim Foundation's aid to Dr. Charles Goddard in his rocket research. They list the many achievements of the medical research supported by the Rockefeller Foundation and point with pride to other foundation-supported initiatives that have resulted in benefiting the public. Nor can anyone deny these achievements.

However, the truth is that these "seed money" ventures are the rare exception rather than the rule. In Waldemar Nielsen's detailed and scholarly study of large foundations, he concludes that only a few desire to assume an innovative role and even the few that do, devote only a small fraction of their total budgets to projects meeting this standard.[10] The role that foundations really play is to sustain already established institutions, not to create new ones. An analysis of total foundation grants shows that established educational institutions receive around 36 percent, health activities over 20 percent, science (which in many cases merely represents another listing for the support of educational institutions) gets a 12 percent slice, and international activities, humanities, and welfare each receive around 10 percent.

When we remember that one of the current objectives of foundations, negative though it may be, is to avoid furnishing government with further grounds for criticism, we can understand why the innovative role is more discussed by public relations officers than by the board members who make decisions. Furthermore, almost without exception, those who constitute the governing boards of the big foundations tend toward conservatism in their political philosophies and prefer maintaining the status quo to embarking on reform programs that could conceivably result in furnishing ammunition to the enemy — whether that enemy consists of government critics or colleagues in the business world. The only logical conclusion that can be reached about the impact of foundations on American philanthropy is that, contrary to the widely held belief, all of them together contribute less than 10 percent of the total given, and the major part of even this small percentage, perhaps as much as 95 percent, goes to established institutions which are by no means solely dependent on the foundations as a source.

CHAPTER 7

Giving for God's Sake

PRUDENT AUTHORS SKIRT or omit entirely any detailed analysis or critique of the vast possessions of the various churches and the billions given to them annually. Early in the preface of the most scholarly book yet published on fund raising, the author warns, "Religious fund raising, which accounts for more than half of American giving, is treated only in a minor way."[1]

The American Association of Fund-Raising Counsel estimates that in 1973 over $10 billion was given to religion. This estimate is simply a well-informed guess, because accurate figures are impossible to obtain. The Protestant denominations to which the majority of Americans belong are a case in point. The National Council of Churches, a coordinating body for many of the Protestant sects, publishes a *Yearbook* with an annual compilation of donations to the various denominations, but it forthrightly admits the inaccuracy of its report: ". . . the U.S. financial data appearing in this section are only a significant part of total contributions from members of all communions. Not all bodies in the U.S. . . . gather church financial data centrally, and some have information but do not reveal it publicly. Additionally, little is known about other major segments of church financial income such as earned income, interest from investments, and bequests." With this caveat, the *Yearbook* discloses that forty-two Protestant bodies with a membership of 42 million persons contributed a total of approximately $4.4 billion, or $104 from the average member. Congregational finances — those expended locally — amounted to $3.6 billion, and benevolences — funds contributed to central parent bodies — totaled $846 million, or about 20 percent of all the funds contributed. The percentage devoted to benevolences varied from as low as 12 percent for some bodies to as high as 46 percent.[2] Figures regarding total investment or the income derived therefrom are unavailable.

No national religious denomination publishes audited figures, but some sects reveal virtually nothing whatever about their finances. The Mormon Church is known to possess real estate of great value in Utah as well as other parts of the U.S. The Church also owns businesses, TV stations, and securities that produce income. The huge new Mormon temple near Washington, D.C., was estimated to cost $15 million, of which one-third was contributed by local congregations, the remainder coming from available church funds.[3]

The Catholic Church is the most tempting subject for study, not because accurate figures are available, but because myth, fantasy, and truth intermingle to create images varying from wealth beyond description all the way to imminent bankruptcy. The shimmering impressions of vast wealth are easy to understand. What is the monetary value of the Vatican, of Chartres, of Seville's magnificent cathedral with its silver altar standing a story high? Coming closer to home, what would be the value at auction of St. Patrick's Cathedral or the University of Notre Dame? Despite these manifestations of vast worldly possessions, the truth is that these irreplaceable testimonials to this faith that has moved men for centuries currently absorb wealth for maintenance rather than create it.

Nevertheless, a number of researchers — some with an anti-Catholic bias and others, although Protestant, truly impartial, but none with Catholic authority — have attempted the unrewarding exercise of evaluating total Catholic wealth in the United States. Despite the difficulties, two scholars, Martin A. Larson and C. Stanley Lowell, conducted research over a five-year period. Their methods of obtaining information rival detective story techniques for ingenuity. They searched real estate tax rolls and stockholder reports, following every local or national lead that might shed light on the subject. In 1969 they estimated American Catholic Church assets at $60 billion, excluding real estate holdings.[4] An earlier book by Dr. Larson estimated the annual income of the Catholic Church in the United States at $13 billion.[5] This is a higher figure than the usual estimated total for all religions. The last official figures published by the U.S. Census Bureau in 1936 placed the value of Catholic churches and rectories at $891.4 million; this figure did not include church-owned hospitals, schools, cemeteries, or other facilities.

The most valuable study of Catholic wealth was conducted by James Gollin and published under the title *Worldly Goods* in 1971. The author, a Protestant, interviewed hundreds of Catholics, lay and clerical, examined thousands of church documents, and emerged with an impressive work of scholarship. He estimates the assets of the Catholic dioceses in the United States at around $25 billion and to this adds about $8 billion in possession of the nearly five hundred religious orders of the Church. Thus Gollin's total for Catholic assets is $33 billion.[6] He also believes that Larson's estimate of Catholic income, $13 billion annually, is 30 percent too high.

If we attempt a completely speculative and non-scholarly estimate, we can take the per capita annual gift of Protestants calculated to be approximately $100[7] and guess that America's 48 million individual Catholics give their church an equal amount, totaling approximately $5 billion a year. Of course, these gifts would not be the church's total income. Fees for marriages, funerals, and other religious ceremonies are not included; nor are proceeds from Bingo games and bazaars in parishes that conduct these forms of fund raising; nor is tuition from the parochial schools; nor are the community fund drives sponsored by the religious groups to finance social welfare agencies; nor is the income on investments held by the dioceses. The only possible conclusion is that an accurate assessment of Catholic income and expenditures is impossible, but this should not prevent us from examining the many areas in which the Church expends these monies.

The confusion attendant on analyzing religious income is perhaps best illustrated when we examine the philanthropic activities of the Jewish minority. There are approximately 6 million Jews in the United States, less than 3 percent of the population. All are Jewish by descent; it does not follow, however, that all are Jewish in religion. Some are Orthodox in their beliefs, following the ancient rituals and ceremonies of their heritage; others belong to Reform synagogues. Many, however, have embraced different religions, usually among the Protestant sects, or follow no organized religion at all. But all are Jews, and nearly all but the very poor, of which happily there are relatively few, contribute to Jewish causes. This giving, because it is not channeled through temples, differs from donations to the Catholic and Protestant churches.

If we separate gifts connected purely with the Jewish religion from those donated toward domestic social causes and aid to Israel, we learn that $23.6 million represented the income of ten national Jewish religious agencies in 1971. These agencies train religious personnel for the future propagation of the faith. However, in the same year, Jews throughout America gave over $350 million to support Jewish-sponsored welfare programs and hospitals, and to aid the development of Israel's social services.[8] Total income from all sources to Jewish-sponsored domestic and overseas programs in 1971 totaled nearly $480 million.

Having estimated, however sketchily, the income for each of the three major religious groupings, we are in a position to examine expenditures. The primary obligation of religious fund raising is the maintenance of places of worship, the replacement of outmoded buildings, and the staffing of these institutions with both religious and lay personnel. As the necessity for religious facilities is dictated by church attendance, it is important to note that in recent years all religions have experienced a steady decline, which is now apparently leveling to a plateau. When the Gallup Poll conducted a scientific sampling of church attendance in 1971, the results indicated that the downward trend of the previous thirteen years was continuing. The largest decline was noted among Roman Catholics, 57 percent of whom attended church in a typical week in 1971 as compared to 71 percent in 1964. Among Protestants and Jews, attendance had remained at approximately the same ratio in the same period, with 37 percent of Protestants and 19 percent of religious Jews attending places of worship in a typical week.

As a result of this drop in attendance, expenditures for new construction of religious buildings have declined steadily in the past decade, particularly when we consider the decreased value of the dollar. The following table illustrates this trend:[9]

Value of New Construction of
Religious Buildings

1965	$1,207,000,000
1967	1,093,000,000
1969	988,000,000
1971	813,000,000
1973	925,000,000

Apart from new construction, only the roughest kind of an estimate can be made as to what proportion of church income is allocated to building maintenance, heating, supplies, and payroll (for clergymen must live even if their compensations are moderate compared to other professions). To cite one non-typical example of the costs of conducting a large cathedral, in 1971 Cardinal Terence Cooke estimated that New York's St. Patrick's Cathedral cost $2100 a day to operate.[10] Obviously, smaller houses of worship cost less; but when we remember the thousands of churches and synagogues that dot America, the total maintenance runs into many millions.

Religiously sponsored education, particularly for the Catholic Church, poses even graver financial problems. The size of this endeavor is indicated by the table below, showing 1968–69 enrollment in elementary and secondary day schools.[11]

Affiliation	Schools	Pupils
Baptist	133	23,671
Christian Reformed	227	45,852
Friends	59	12,169
Jewish	302	66,724
Lutheran	1,394	195,690
Methodist	50	5,374
Presbyterian	38	4,732
Protestant Episcopal	319	54,122
Roman Catholic	12,343	4,843,188
Seventh-Day Adventist	787	51,588

As the scope of the Catholic effort surpasses those of all the other faiths put together, the financial implications are of particular interest, and the National Catholic Educational Association regularly makes some figures available on the amount of support furnished by the Church.[12] In Catholic elementary schools in 1972–73, the total cost per pupil was $280 per year. Of this sum, about $90 came from tuition. The largest subsidy, $144, came from parish funds; dioceses contributed $5.44, and the central church $1.00. At the secondary school level, for those high schools classified as parish-diocesan schools, the cost per pupil was $575 per year. Tuition averaged $325, the parish subsidy $75, the diocesan subsidy $73, and the church subsidy only $.24. (These figures do not balance only because I have omitted small amounts of other income from fees and gifts.) For the so-called private secondary schools under general church supervision rather than parish or diocesan control, the cost per student was $852 per year, of which tuition paid $664, diocesan subsidy $8, and church $21. Multiplying the nearly 5 million students by these various categories of parish, diocesan, and church subsidies gives the answer to where the dollars contributed on Sundays are spent on the other days of the week.

The parochial school system is creating a serious financial dilemma for the Catholic Church. A number of economic factors, which are currently combining, threaten the very future of this religiously oriented education. Middle-class Catholics are deserting urban centers for the suburbs, leaving only those city dwellers who can least afford even the moderate tuitions. With declining enrollment in Catholic seminaries, the number of religious, be they nuns or priests, available as teachers is declining sharply. Each lay teacher hired as a substitute receives compensation far in excess of that provided religious personnel. Finally, inflation is raising all costs at the very time that many people's incomes are declining. Here is one form of philanthropy that, under the Constitution, government cannot assist, and despite determined efforts to solicit government aid under any guise that would be legal, substantial assistance from this source is unlikely. Catholics warn that if they are forced to discontinue the parochial schools, the public schools will be inundated by additional children. In some locations with very high Catholic density, this might be true. However, given the declining birth rate and lowered school attendance in many areas, gradual absorption should be possible in the event that individual parishes are forced to close or consolidate their schools.[13]

Of the 2626 institutions of higher learning in the United States in 1971–72, 1152 were public and 1474 private. Of the private institutions, 671 had no religious affiliation, 489 were Protestant, 275 Catholic, and the remaining 39 were of miscellaneous faiths. Of these religious colleges or universities, 80 percent identified themselves as "church controlled," while the remaining 20 percent described themselves as "church affiliated."[14]

Fiscal examination of the Catholic affiliated colleges is facilitated by a comprehensive study entitled *The Independent Catholic College*, prepared by the National Catholic Educational Association.[15] Enrollment in the 275 traditionally Catholic colleges was 451,000 students in 1970–71. The faculties consisted of 71 percent full-time teachers, 47 percent with master's and 46 percent with doctorate degrees. As to revenue, all the institutions combined just about balanced income and expenditure. A surprising fact emerged from the report: "Church support is a negligible revenue factor (.2%)."

This statement is explained on examining the individual financial statements of a number of Church-affiliated colleges. The great Catholic universities are open and generous in furnishing interested people with complete audited annual reports: the five from which I requested information — Boston College, Holy Cross, Fordham, Georgetown, and Notre Dame — sent audited reports promptly. (Except for Notre Dame, these institutions are conducted by the Jesuit order.)

Examining the detailed report of one of these institutions, Boston College, discloses facts that apply generally to the others. During the years of 1967–71, expenditures at B.C. exceeded revenues. In recent years, the budget has been brought into balance and a small surplus has resulted. Tuition and fees furnish 65 percent of all income. The Catholic Church contributes nothing whatever to this institution. This absence of support permits government to sponsor massive research projects, and in 1972 the federal government granted $5.5 million, the state $229,000, and the local government $91,000 to B.C. One aspect of its operation distinguishes it from lay colleges. All members of the faculty receive salaries consonant with their scholarly attainments and the rates paid by other institutions in the area; however, those faculty members who belong to the learned Jesuit order, having taken an oath of poverty, return their stipend as a gift to the college.

While most of the better-known Catholic-affiliated universities are completely independent of financial support from the Church, the Catholic Church itself conducts a declining number of seminaries for training in the priesthood. In 1962, 545 of these institutions existed, with a combined enrollment of 46,000 students. By 1973, there were only 411 seminaries, with an enrollment of 22,000.[16] The Catholic University of America in Washington, D.C., founded around 1880, is the only institution for general education supported by the central Catholic Church in the United States.[17]

Institutions of higher education affiliated with the Protestants or Jews do not, for the most part, receive direct church support. This is generally true of the colleges loosely affiliated with Protestant sects, though various Protestant denominations do conduct seminaries and theological schools; in 1971, there were 187 such institutions with a total enrollment of 32,750.[18] Deficits at such universities as Brandeis or Yeshiva are met by philanthropy from the Jewish community, not by any central body.

All of the major religions sponsor various welfare activities quite apart from their educational institutions. However, funds to support these agencies do not flow through churches but are raised by sectarian campaigns organized in many major cities. In New York, for example, the Catholic Charities of the Archdiocese of New York had an income of approximately $5.2 million in 1972. Of this amount, $3.3 million resulted from the annual fund appeal, $121,000 was contributed by the non-sectarian Greater New York Fund, $438,000 derived from legacies, and $1.3 million from sundry income. In 1971, the Federation of Jewish Philanthropies, which supports local welfare agencies, collected $23.8 million in New York City. The United Jewish Appeal, which distributes funds for various social purposes in Israel, raised $73 million. The Federation of Protestant Welfare Agencies received $1.3 million in New York City in 1973.

While it may be straining a definition to describe sectarian fund raising for hospitals, child care centers, and homes for the aged as religious, there is no doubt that loyalty to the various faiths furnishes the emotional stimulus required to make these annual campaigns successful. The major voluntary hospitals sponsored by the various faiths no longer require philanthropic support except for capital expenditures, nor are they sectarian with regard to patients or staff. The government furnishes most of the funds required to conduct the child care agencies and much of what is needed for other welfare activities. Nevertheless, sectarian fund raising follows the general rule of non-sectarian effort; namely, that funds continue to be raised, regardless of need, as long as people are willing to give.

As for the amount of religious funds raised in America that are exported for various purposes, figures have been made available only by the Jews, who have published data concerning the massive aid to Israel contributed in American cities with substantial Jewish populations. From 1948 through 1971, the United Jewish Appeal, the largest fundraising organization for this purpose, provided $1.7 billion to aid projects in Israel. Other agencies contributed lesser funds for educational or other specified purposes.[19] Various Protestant sects sponsor missionary activity all over the world, involving personnel, supplies, and often welfare aid, but the total financial scope of this effort is impossible to ascertain. The Catholic Church exports money to Rome to assist in the maintenance of the Vatican and to permit expanded activities and missions in Catholic countries with less affluent populations. The annual Peter's Pence collection in all dioceses is the most widely known fount of this support, but the totals of this collection are not published. I have seen estimates which range up to $1 billion a year as to the total amount exported, but it could be half that amount or far less so far as anyone really knows outside of the highest councils of the Church. The Vatican is not dependent upon contributions from abroad for survival, because wise investment policies of the $90 million paid by the Italian government in 1929, when papal lands were taken over, assures adequate maintenance for the Pope and his staff.

The scope of religious philanthropy in the United States is easy to underestimate. The commonly accepted allocation is 43 percent of total philanthropic giving, which is probably a fairly accurate estimate of annual contributions. However, fees for services, tuition, interest on investment, and other income quite apart from gifts swell the total spending for religious causes to a far larger figure, probably more than half of the voluntary total for all philanthropic causes.

The strongest attachment formed by religiously oriented people of every belief is — outside of family and close friends — that to their faith. The act of giving is prompted much more by emotion than by any coldly rational process, and from time immemorial people have responded to the appeals for support of their religious faith. Historically, most charity was dispensed through churches; so a gift was not only a spiritual offering but represented alms for the poor as well. Today, much is being written about the weakening of religious ties in our country; but if the flow of gifts is a valid criterion, religious causes continue to maintain the highest priority.

CHAPTER 8

Children Are Good Fund Raisers

THE PLIGHT of the helpless child, whether orphaned, abandoned, or crippled, touches adult hearts. Tear-jerking photographs of hungry waifs stare out from advertisements with an accompanying fund appeal assuring that a modest gift would assist these suffering innocents. Sometimes the photographs are real; sometimes they are doctored. One agency used for six years a pathetic picture of a five-year-old boy who the text said was starving. In truth, the picture was that of a twelve-year-old girl who was not starving but was being supported by an Ohio couple.[1] Another agency admitted that it had drawn composite portraits of children in its advertisements and had not always used correct names.[2] Still another conceded that a school in Hong Kong received funds in 1974 for support of children who had left the school in the middle of the previous year.[3] In fairness, the government agency that uncovered these frauds conceded that all three of the cited organizations did some good work with the money they received.

Meeting children's needs includes so many activities that a definition narrowing the scope for the following discussion is helpful. The Advisory Council on Child Welfare (U.S. Department of Health, Education and Welfare) defines child welfare as follows:

> Those social services that supplement or substitute for parental care and supervision for the purpose of protecting and promoting the welfare of children and youth, preventing neglect and abuse and exploitation, helping overcome problems that result in dependency and neglect or delinquency and where needed providing adequate care for children and youth away from their own homes, such care to be given in foster family homes, adoptive homes, child caring institutions or other facilities.

A great deal of money and hard work would be required to alleviate the problems of America's hapless children — far too much to be provided by means of even an infinite number of emotional appeals to compassionate donors. Today there are approximately 70 million Americans under eighteen years of age. Only about 0.1 percent, or 70,000, have lost both parents and are orphans in the literal sense.[4] This low figure marks great progress, for in 1920 orphans made up 16.3 percent of the child population.[5] Despite this reduction, by 1970 some 3 million children required social services from welfare agencies: 300,000 were receiving foster care and nearly 100,000 were in adoptive homes.[6] According to a study done in 1965, about 39 out of every 1000 children under eighteen at the time had been born out of wedlock. About 1 out of 6 youths between the ages of sixteen and twenty-one was out of school and out of work. About 17 percent of the popula-

tion under fifteen had some physically crippling condition; 8 to 15 percent of all school-age children were
estimated to be emotionally disturbed. Over 1 percent of
all children between the ages of ten and seventeen had
been involved in delinquency cases in juvenile courts.[7] As
of 1970 there were more than 7 million young people who
were emotionally disturbed, mentally retarded, physically
handicapped, or suffering special learning difficulties.
Many were poor, most were not; but nearly 5 million of
them could get no help.[8] This dreary catalogue of needs
could be lengthened interminably.

It is virtually impossible to estimate the total sum that is
spent by government and philanthropy on all phases of
child care, but expenditures are in the billions. Certain
specific figures illustrate the magnitude of the needs. It
has been estimated that an infant who entered the foster
care system in New York City and has remained in it for
the full eighteen years of childhood will have cost the
staggering total of $122,500. This contrasts with an esti-
mate of $25,560 for the cost of rearing a child over the
same period in his own home.[9] To cite an extreme case,
the cost of caring for a difficult teen-ager in an institution
adequately staffed to handle this type of case can run as
high as $24,000 for just one year. It is abundantly clear
from these figures that if our society put as much emphasis
on keeping families together as it does on caring for children who are unwanted or uncared for, tremendous sums
could be saved. The present welfare system, which
rewards the deserted mother, encourages the division of
families.

Adoption is the most obvious way of assuring that an

unwanted child will be brought up in a family home. A multitude of organizations, both voluntary and governmental, exist to assist in adoption procedures. Just a list of the various legitimate adoptive agencies in the fifty states, with a brief description of the purposes of each, takes up 122 pages of small print.[10] There is little trouble in finding homes for physically and mentally normal white children; indeed, there is a waiting list of applicants who wish to adopt them. In contrast, black children, particularly in large cities with ghetto populations, are more difficult to place. There is an insufficient number of middle-class black families willing to take on the economic burden of an additional child. Furthermore, because unemployment is high and incomes low among urban blacks, there is a disproportionately large number of children requiring foster care.

In meeting the huge financial needs of the country's many child welfare programs, government's role is constantly increasing and philanthropy's declining. Today, all the nation's voluntary agencies put together receive about half their incomes from government; some receive up to 100 percent. When most of the voluntary agencies were organized, caring for abandoned children was entirely the responsibility of philanthropy. As needs were recognized and became greater, government funding became increasingly necessary. It would have been wasteful madness for government to disregard the fine institutions and excellent staffs recruited by the voluntary agencies; so the logical course of government subsidy became the pattern in localities where these facilities existed.

In a 1973 survey of some 200 voluntary child care agencies throughout the United States, total non-government funds came to $72 million, or just over half the total income. Of this amount, nearly $40 million came from federated funds, $33 million from the United Way, and $7 million from sectarian fund-raising efforts. Government support varies greatly by region as do expenditures for child care. In the Middle Atlantic states, which include New York, 77 percent of all income for these voluntary agencies came from government; in the center of the South, government's share was only 6 percent. Despite this wide variation, in all regions income from government and federated funds together ranged between 62 and 90 percent of the total.[11] As can readily be seen, direct gifts to the agencies from individuals amounted to a very small part of the total. Of course, all the money disbursed by the voluntary agencies was only a small percentage of the total expended on child care by the states and municipalities in the programs they conducted.

With government funds available to meet the most pressing needs, the question arises whether philanthropy still has any valid role to play in the child care field. Those who espouse pluralism contend that voluntary programs, unhindered by red tape, can initiate advanced programs with far more ease than can government. However, knowledgeable social workers have told me that, in recent years, government agencies have actually been more innovative in child welfare than the voluntary ones. In this activity, as in so many other philanthropic areas, once an organization is created to do a specific job, its leaders tend to become more interested in maintaining the organization than in providing the service it was designed to perform.

Despite the declining need for philanthropic activity in the direct care of children, one important function continues to be entirely dependent on non-governmental funds: in an endeavor in which vast sums are expended and results are far from perfect, there is need for continuing evaluation of performance and suggestions for remedial reform. Operating agencies cannot evaluate their own work impartially; government's lack of self-criticism is axiomatic. The Child Welfare League of America, founded in 1920, is a coordinating agency with a membership of some three hundred child care agencies. It is maintained entirely by non-governmental funds contributed as dues by the member organizations, gifts, grants from foundations, and an allocation from the United Fund. The League outlines its own program in its literature:

> It develops standards for service; it conducts research; it provides consultation to agencies and communities; it publishes professional materials; it works with national and international organizations to improve policies affecting the welfare of children, and it provides legislative groups with the information necessary for the passage of sound legislation.

With an annual budget of around $1.5 million, this agency conducts a needed program.

Local agencies with similar objectives exist in some of our major cities. In New York, for example, the Citizens' Committee for Children maintains a vigilance over both governmental and voluntary agencies that deal with chil-

dren. The program includes surveillance of the juvenile
courts, lawsuits affecting children's rights, and legislative
action. A similar body has been formed in Buffalo. These
agencies, important as they are, have a serious fund-
raising problem. Donors want to give directly to agencies
caring for or curing children. There is little emotional
appeal in the endless work of conducting surveys, suggest-
ing reforms, and criticizing current programs. Nonetheless, money donated to this type of agency has more
impact today than similar amounts given to direct care
agencies.

While the needs for philanthropic financing have declined sharply in the child welfare field, recreational
activity still attracts major voluntary support. Government at every level spends vast sums creating and maintaining recreational facilities. From huge national parks
such as Yellowstone and Yosemite and state-maintained
forests right down to municipal swimming pools and play-
grounds, including public school athletic fields and village
recreational programs, government provides varied areas
where youth can play. However, in contrast to the child
welfare field, government contributes little or nothing to
the voluntary agencies that conduct group activities to
utilize these resources.

The Boy Scouts of America, for example, is a country-
wide organization consisting of a national headquarters,
local councils that supervise scouting in their areas, and
local membership units. The national headquarters received about $13 million in a recent year; the councils had
an income of $92 million, of which about 80 percent came

from the United Way, and the local units raised additional funds with their small dues. In short, perhaps $120 million total was expended in this program. When this figure is compared to the previously cited $72 million given to some 200 voluntary child care organizations, a concrete comparison of the relative magnitude of philanthropy in the two areas emerges. A few years ago only about 3 percent of inner-city boys were enrolled in scout troops. Recently, scout executives have made a major effort with both money and volunteers to enlist ghetto children. Chief Scout Executive Alden G. Barber points to the success of this crash program by claiming that four times as many ghetto children have joined troops as belonged previously. But most of these troops are paper units, which quickly fall apart for lack of community involvement. Even though many children join, most soon drop out of the program. The cost of scouting equipment, the lack of wildlife or even trees in urban ghettos, and the character-building platitudes that have been part of the scouting ritual since the organization's inception in 1910 all combine to make the program irrelevant to the poor. It is nearly impossible to think of a way in which the scouting program harms any of the 5 million participating boys, but I find it nearly as difficult to see the current benefits of teaching the historic survival and handicraft skills of our frontier heritage to boys living in the most highly industrialized country in the world.

The Girl Scouts derive about three quarters of their income of $10 million from membership dues, and the 3 million girls that participate, as well as the nearly 700,000 volunteer leaders, come largely from middle-class suburban families. The Camp Fire Girls, with a membership of over 600,000, have a proportionately lower budget. The 4-H Clubs are a type of rural equivalent, but one that is more utilitarian, in its vocational training of young farmers, than is scouting. Government funds are available for many aspects of 4-H's educational program, but a foundation with a budget of $2 million coordinates and assists with training programs.

Servicing an older age group, the YMCA, supported by voluntary financing, has extensive facilities in many of the nation's cities. The Young Men's Christian Association was formed in London in 1844 by some salesmen in a London store "to improve the spiritual condition of young men engaged in the drapery trades." The idea came to America in the 1850s, and bodily health was added to spiritual development as a goal. Over the decades of its growth, the organization has developed a chain of facilities for men's athletics, group meetings, and dormitories.[12] Despite its name, the YMCA accepts girls and women as members, and people of any religious faith may join. Only about half of the members are under eighteen. Nearly 6 million individuals are enrolled members and another 2 million use the equipment. The YMCA began as a middle-class endeavor and has remained so, though recently a sincere effort has been mounted to develop programs for lower-income groups in urban centers. YMCA facilities are continuing to multiply, with twenty-three new buildings completed in 1973 alone, at a cost of over $12 million. Each year some 150 building renovations or additions are undertaken at an estimated cost of around $150 million. It is interesting to note that the YMCA's recent development has followed the migration of the middle class to the suburbs. In the last twenty years, three out of four new Y buildings have been erected in the suburbs or residential areas of cities. The facilities that the Y's offer differ greatly, depending on local support. Some have swimming pools, squash courts, and elaborate athletic equipment, as well as dormitories, available for moderate fees. Others are far less pretentious. In the Washington area, for example, the YMCA conducts eleven branches but only two are in the District itself. The main branch, two blocks from the White House, is one of the more elaborate. The other branch, in a poorer black district, offers far less; as of 1970 the swimming pool facilities had not been in operation for years, and the basketball court was serviceable only in daylight, because of inadequate lighting. The YMCA receives considerable funds from the United Way, and membership dues, fees, gifts, and bequests maintain the program. The YMCA is by far the largest endeavor of its kind, but the Young Women's Christian Association, which celebrated its hundredth birthday in 1970, and the Young Men's and Young Women's Hebrew Associations conduct similar if less extensive programs on a national scale.

In our cities, a large number of settlement houses and community centers under voluntary sponsorship conduct group programs for youth. Some of these local institutions, like Chicago's Hull House and New York's Henry Street Settlement, have achieved national fame for their longevity and fine work. No vast national organization such as the Scouts or the Y's exists to supervise these local efforts, but a coordinating agency, the National Federation

of Settlements and Neighborhood Centers, exists in New
York City to provide advice and research for its member
agencies. While all these institutions provide group activities under trained leadership, their programs vary widely,
depending on community needs. After visiting well over
100 of these institutions in many cities and states, a
scholar in the social work field wrote a book describing the
wide range of varying programs.[13] These agencies receive a large proportion of their funds from philanthropy,
although government has increasingly assisted in financing programs designed to reduce narcotic addiction and
juvenile delinquency.

Philanthropy also supports a recreational program for
our armed service personnel. The United Service Organization, started just before the outbreak of World War II,
has continuously offered various forms of entertainment to
the military forces. With today's volunteer army, the USO
has broadened its scope to develop programs in the areas of
drug abuse and service to minority groups. It is joined in
this effort by the Y's, the National Catholic Community
Service, the Salvation Army, and the National Jewish
Welfare Board.

Programs relating to children and youth furnish an excellent case study of general philanthropic trends and
development. Responsibility for the financing of the abso-
lutely essential functions in child care and welfare have
passed from philanthropy to government. On the other
hand, the less essential, but enjoyable and enriching programs for recreation are still largely supported by voluntary gifts. It would appear that the trend will continue,

with philanthropy's financial responsibility for child care steadily diminishing. I asked a professor of social work at Columbia (who prefers to remain unidentified because her work involves continuing contact with voluntary agencies that would certainly not agree with her assessment), "What do you see as the future role of philanthropy in the child care field?" Without hesitation she replied, "None, none whatsoever."

CHAPTER 9

The Overneedy Hospitals

OUR SOCIETY REQUIRES no institutions more urgently than hospitals. Without schools, we would be uneducated; without hospitals, we would be dead. People want to give money to improve health care, and hospitals are the central agencies for its distribution. United Fund campaigns as well as other federated drives such as United Hospital Funds stress the financial dilemmas faced by hospitals, and the implication is clear that philanthropy is necessary for the survival of these great medical centers. There is only one flaw in this simplistic picture; it is not true. Hospitals unquestionably do face financial problems, but they are of a magnitude beyond philanthropy's resources.

Most of America's voluntary hospitals were originally established by groups of rich men who donated sufficient funds to erect the necessary central structures. Those patients who could pay did so. The deficits created by those who could not pay were met by philanthropy. As medical science advanced and costs increased, insurance plans such as Blue Cross evolved to meet the middle class's desire and ability to pay for its own hospital care through modest premiums paid periodically. Simultaneously, governmental subdivisions, states, municipalities, and even towns partially reimbursed hospitals when they admitted indigent patients. As both Blue Cross allowances and the governmental stipends were below the actual costs incurred by the hospitals, philanthropy was called upon to meet the deficits. In recent years, however, and particularly following the passage of Medicare and Medicaid, both insurance plan payments and governmental compensation were calculated to reimburse actual hospital costs so that, except in extraordinary and short-lived circumstances, deficits no longer occurred. This evolution, while well known to those directly concerned with hospital administration, was not widely publicized.

The era of total reimbursement for all costs lifted financial worries from the backs of hospital administrators, but, like many by-products of affluence, it had a damaging side effect. It eliminated the most important pressure for expense control. When boards of trustees had been responsible for furnishing the funds to meet a deficit, even though that figure was a small percentage of total expenditures, administrators proceeded with caution before incurring additional losses. After such deficits were eliminated by total reimbursement, hospital costs climbed faster than any other segment of the cost of living.

A large proportion of this upward spiral was long overdue. As in most philanthropic endeavor, the wages prevailing in hospitals were a disgrace. Workers were making a contribution to philanthropy, although in many cases their income levels were so low that they should have been its recipients instead. With the total reimbursement formulas, these wages shot upward to or even past the levels prevailing in industry for similar tasks. With the unionization of hospital workers in a number of cities, particularly New York, and with the threat of labor organization hanging over hospitals in other localities, the total labor costs, which amount to some 70 percent of the average hospital's expenditures, skyrocketed. Unlike industry, which makes an effort to link productivity to wage increases, hospitals had evolved no method of measuring worker productivity. Not only did wages rise, but more employees were added as the new, competitive salary levels made recruitment easier. According to the American Hospital Association, in 1946 the voluntary non-profit hospitals in the United States employed the equivalent, including part-timers, of 156 full-time people to serve each 100 patients. By 1963, there were comparably 244 full-time employees per 100 patients — and in New York in the same year 261 full-time personnel served each 100 patients. Today the figure is nearly 300 employees for each 100 patients. Experts explaining this increase cite the more complicated procedures, requiring additional personnel, that have resulted from advancing medical knowledge.

During the period when Blue Cross and government reimbursed hospitals for all their losses, the boards of trustees surrendered their control over increasing expenses. An imaginary conversation between a board chairman and the hospital's professional administrator might have gone something like this:

Chairman of Board: Our nursing costs have risen out of sight. We must cut down on the number of nurses.

Administrator: We can cut down if you insist. Just give me a signed memo on how many patients you are willing to kill to save nursing costs.

Chairman of Board: You mean we can't cut down without killing people?

Administrator: My professional opinion is that we are still understaffed. Any reduction in nursing coverage would inevitably reduce the quality of patient care. Besides, we will be completely reimbursed for our added costs.

The upward pressure on expenses came from the medical staff as well as the administration. One conscientious hospital executive took the chief doctor of his radiology department to task for an increase in film expenses of 50 percent. The doctor's response was that he had concrete evidence that by taking 50 percent more exposures he found one additional case of cancer of the lung in every 10,000 patients. The executive, in the absence of accepted guidelines or stringent cost control, felt himself helpless to counter the argument.

The halcyon days of financial plenty for hospitals came to an end in the early 1970s. Doctors' fees as well as hospital costs spiraled upward, and impecunious patients who could drag themselves to outpatient clinics thronged to these hospital facilities. Between 1963 and 1973, total annual outpatient visits increased from 118 to 234 million.[1] Neither Blue Cross nor Medicaid reimbursed the hospitals for these visits, each of which cost the institution about $40. Patients who could afford it paid; most could not. Added to this factor was the rising costs of all the materials hospitals require — food, paper, medicines, dressings, and, most of all, labor. Deficits became catastrophic. Journalists ran headline articles blazoning such succinct messages as "Why the Nation's Hospitals May Well Go Broke."[2] Even such well-heeled hospitals as New York's Columbia Presbyterian went through its $12 million unrestricted endowment funds in little over a year. Other hospitals were forced to borrow money at high interest rates. The president of the American Hospital Association admits that many large city hospitals are beyond relief by either philanthropy or even greater rate increases. He adds that nothing short of a complete revision in financing health care with government underwriting will reverse the situation.[3]

Almost to prove the thesis that philanthropic fund raising will continue for any cause so long as funds flow, United Funds and United Hospital Funds continue to stress hospitals' dependence on gifts. Those responsible for preparing this kind of publicity must know that counting on philanthropic contributions to offset huge hospital deficits is equivalent to trying to put out a three-alarm fire with a bucket brigade. The United Hospital Fund of New York was originally organized in 1879 as the Hospital Saturday and Sunday Association "to obtain benevolent gifts for hospitals of New York . . . also to further economy in management and to co-ordinate and extend the work of hospitals." So long as hospitals required philanthropic income to meet their operating deficits, the United Hospital Fund performed a useful function in conducting a non-sectarian fund-raising appeal each year. Corporations and individuals contributed as a result of a well-organized solicitation that put particular emphasis on pressuring those companies having a trustee of some hospital as the chief executive or at least in a position of power. In 1969, more than $5.5 million was collected, of which $3.5 million was distributed by a complex formula to some fifty-nine hospitals. Obviously, the proportionate amount received by each hospital was trivial. To be specific, one hospital with a total operating budget of nearly $80 million received $40,000 after filing time-consuming reports and preparing meaningless budget documents to accommodate the Fund's distribution criteria. The fund-raising effort cost $500,000 in expenses and another $400,000 for administrative costs. Another $500,000 was spent by the Fund performing various research services that, while supposed to be of value to member hospitals, are in fact of dubious merit. Thus $1.5 million of the $5.5 million total was spent in one way or another by the collecting agency, and only $4 million went to hospitals.

Will the United Hospital Fund terminate its efforts? Of course not. Too many jobs are at stake, too many people occupy at least some of their time collecting for this once worthy cause. Recently the United Hospital Fund merged with the Greater New York United Fund, but by any logic both Funds should stop soliciting support for hospitals.

Due to fund-raising propaganda, the public still believes that hospitals require philanthropic funds — and for one purpose they still do. Government does not provide all funds for new construction. With proper authorization, the federal government will pay up to two thirds of the cost of needed new facilities, but even in these cases it is necessary for philanthropy to raise one-third. The requirement that philanthropy need pay only one third of the cost of a new building creates the opportunity for major donors to have large buildings named for them at what amounts to a 66 percent discount. Thus we have seen a proliferation of pavilions, nurses' dormitories, laboratories, and other hospital facilities, each with a donor's name carved over the entrance. In most instances the benefactor footed one third of the bill. To understand fully the bargain of giving a major hospital building, we must also recall that large donors are usually in the 70 percent tax bracket and thus do not pay income taxes on over two thirds of the money they give. The major donor can build his memorial to himself or his family for one third of one third — or one ninth — of its total construction cost. Small wonder that fund raisers for hospitals are often successful in their quest for capital construction funds.

Even regarding hospital construction, philanthropy's role is steadily decreasing. There are some eighteen federal programs which provide capital funds in addition to money available under the Hill-Burton law, which is being phased out. Twenty-three states have programs to aid hospital projects: seven have already issued tax-exempt hospital bonds; and a dozen more have created authorities to issue such bonds. In 1968, philanthropy furnished 24.2 percent of the funds used in hospital construction projects. By 1969 the figure had declined to 17.9 percent and in 1973 it amounted to only 11.7 percent.[4] There is not the slightest doubt that the trend will continue downward.

Donors will continue wanting to give to hospitals, just as they wanted to help the poor long after it was readily apparent that the nation's poverty was far too massive a problem to be solved by voluntary gifts. Fund-raising organizations will dutifully accommodate this desire by stressing the dire need posed by hospital financing. But philanthropic funds, except those marked for special research projects or for construction, cannot serve even as a palliative to the dilemma. Nothing short of a revision in the government's funding of health care will provide access for all citizens to the medical care that is available, but beyond the economic grasp of too many Americans.

CHAPTER 10

The Health Agencies Live on Death

THE COMMON EXPERIENCE of losing loved ones by disease or through frailties of the human body activates those compassionate emotions that result in a flow of philanthropic dollars into the general area of health improvement. Virtually every specific disease, from alcoholism to tuberculosis, has a voluntary agency dedicated to combating its ravages. In addition, those organs of the body most susceptible to disease — eyes, ears, heart, kidneys, teeth — have philanthropic defenders determined to ward off afflictions. Nor do these two armies march alone, for in addition there are smaller organizations dedicated to the health problems of special groups such as children, expectant mothers, the aged, the mentally retarded. Furthermore, an organization consisting largely of professionals, the American Public Health Association, exists to improve the distribution and availability of health care for all. This group sponsors programs for improving medical education, expanding nursing care, establishing better public health facilities, and disseminating health information of a general nature to the public.

One would suspect that such a highly splintered approach to health problems would breed duplication of effort and inefficiency of administration — and it does. But the reason for the burgeoning number of health agencies, each approaching the problem from a different direction, has its own logic if we keep in mind that in all philanthropic effort a sufficiency of funds and the ability to raise them outrank the dictates of an orderly approach. Fund-raising specialists mount massive campaigns simultaneously stressing advances in medical knowledge and warning of still current dangers. Thus hope and fear combine to encourage people to join the crusade by giving money or by performing volunteer work in the fight against the disease that robbed them of their loved one.

The magnitude of the human effort contributed to the health agencies is impressive and increases from decade to decade. In 1945 there existed 20,000 such agencies supported by some 300,000 people serving as volunteers or as members of boards of trustees.[1] By 1961, according to a report sponsored by the Rockefeller Foundation, there were 100,000 voluntary health and welfare agencies in addition to another 100,000 fraternal, civic, veterans', and related organizations that sponsored some health and welfare activities as a part of their programs.[2] While these totals are impressive, many of the agencies included were tiny, strictly local in scope, and limited in their objectives by small budgets.

In 1973, thirty-six national voluntary health agencies raised nearly $500 million. (Just twelve of the largest agencies raised approximately $300 million.) While these are large figures, they are dwarfed by government's expenditures in the same fields. For fiscal 1974, Congress appropriated $3.3 billion for parallel programs conducted by the National Institutes of Health and other government agencies. Tables listing the income and monies expended for research by the largest voluntary agencies are included in the appendices, as are parallel tables showing incidence of varying diseases and government appropriations (see Appendices B1, B2, B3, pp. 172 through 175).

With such a myriad of separate agencies and with compassion rather than actual need the basis for financial support, it is hardly surprising that various individuals and commissions have recommended structural reform, consolidation, and elimination of duplication. Soon after World War II, Selskar M. Gunn and Philip S. Platt studied the then existing voluntary health agencies in great detail. These authors recognized that a single-interest agency focused on a broad area is more likely both to achieve its objectives and to attract sufficient funds than many separate agencies. The single-interest agency also avoids the scramble for gifts that is the inevitable result when there are many disparate organizations, each with competing appeals. Resistance to unity arises in the case of the agency that has successfully mounted fund-raising campaigns for a disease that afflicts a relatively small percentage of the population. For example, right up to the time the vaccine for polio was discovered, the National Foundation, as a policy matter, always declined to join others, because the agency was able to raise the largest sums of any organization for a disease that afflicted only 1 person in 30,000. Another deterrent to unification is that many volunteers and board members would lose interest if their pet cause were submerged in a general fund. Despite these arguments, dictated mostly by emotional and fund-raising considerations, Gunn and Platt recommended a major unified health agency with the broad objectives of generally improving health, through a careful study of the needs, and closing existing gaps caused by lack of overall planning. Despite the obvious soundness of these recommendations, consolidation did not occur. Indeed, further splintering and duplication proliferated in the following thirty years.

In 1961, after over a year's study, an ad hoc commission sponsored by the Rockefeller Foundation issued a report on the strengths and shortcomings of the voluntary health agencies. This commission made two major recommendations, both aimed toward improving cooperation and coordination between the multiplying agencies. The first suggestion was that a major commission of knowledgeable citizens be formed to study and evaluate the performances of existing agencies and to recommend methods of eliminating duplication, filling in gaps overlooked by all existing agencies, and establishing methods of achieving cooperation in fund raising as well as in program activities. The second recommendation was that all health agencies should adopt uniform accounting procedures so that meaningful comparative studies could be made in such shadowy areas as the expense of fund raising, cost of administration, and expenditures for public information and general publicity.[3] Only this second recommendation achieved a limited degree of acceptance. When, in 1969, I inquired of Dr. Robert H. Hamlin, the study director for this commission, as to the concrete results of his report, he stated that uniform accounting had been adopted by the nineteen major voluntary health agencies belonging to the National Health Council, which acts as a general forum.[4] As to the other recommendation for an overhaul of the whole field, no more action occurred than had followed the earlier Gunn-Platt critique. In view of the continued insistence by the individual agencies on maintaining their separate identities, it would seem that any hopes for a monolithic voluntary agency in the health field exist only in the minds of reformers who view the general situation objectively.

If disease in any form were not so inherently tragic, the overlapping, the duplication, the misplaced priorities, and just the plain waste of money demonstrated by the voluntary health agencies would be a perfect subject for satire. For those who advocate pluralism in our society, here is pluralism to the point of lunacy.

As a case in point, there is the American Cancer Society, the largest of any of the voluntary health agencies, with an income of nearly $100 million a year. Quite separate from it are the Cancer Research Institute, the Runyon-Winchell Cancer Fund, and the Leukemia Society. These smaller agencies together raise another $10 million a year. The United States government expends $555 million annually in its efforts to find causes and cures for this disease. And with all this, cancer is by no means the principle cause of death in the U.S.

The government spends nearly $800 million annually on the general category of mental health. Here again there are multiple voluntary agencies working in the same field — among them, the National Association for Mental Health, the American Schizophrenia Association, and countless local philanthropic efforts to assist retarded children.

Each of three organs of the human body has an association of its own. The American Heart Association is second only to the American Cancer Society as the largest voluntary agency. Cardiovascular diseases are the greatest cause of death in this country, with a death rate of 494 per 100,000 as compared with cancer's 167, but the Heart Association raises only two-thirds as much as the Cancer Society does. The kidneys and the lungs are also each represented by a national association.

When we look to the diseases that have organized philanthropic combatants, we are reminded of the curriculum of a medical school. Alcoholism, allergies, arthritis, birth defects, blindness, cerebral palsy, cystic fibrosis, deafness, diabetes, epilepsy, hemophilia, multiple sclerosis, muscular dystrophy, myasthenia gravis, and Parkinson's disease — each has a separate organization to fight its ravages. The venereal diseases are all dealt with by the Social Health Association. If I have omitted any in this listing, it has been inadvertent.

Facts establish what logic would lead us to believe; i.e., that the splintered approach to disease control is inefficient and wasteful. Even a cursory examination raises grave questions about the huge totals expended each year by the voluntary health agencies just to raise the funds which support their programs. Again, let us take the largest as example, the American Cancer Society. Here is an agency that performs much fine work, attracts thousands of dedicated volunteers, makes many grants to important research, and annually publishes its audited financial statement for anyone interested to examine. In 1973, the Society raised some $63 million from living people (this does not include $17 million in bequests). Its fund-raising and administrative expenses totaled $17 million. Some $24 million was spent in research programs. But perhaps the most interesting figure is the $7.5 million excess income over total expenditures. This sum was added to the already huge amount of the Society's total assets (over $100 million), most of which was invested in interest-yielding securities. Yet one of the appeals that the Cancer Society makes in its fund-raising literature is that it is forced to turn down many deserving applications for research grants. Why? Incidentally, while these figures are large, the National Institute of Health devotes twenty-five times as much to cancer research as does the voluntary agency.

When we examine the operation of the Easter Seal Society for Crippled Children and Adults, there is considerably more reason for criticism. This organization raised $53 million in 1972. Most Americans are familiar with the advertisements prior to the annual spring fund-raising campaign that picture a wistfully smiling child weighed down by unsightly leg braces. Presumably, we are being asked for donations to help such children recover the use of their limbs. One of the fund-raising methods this agency uses is to send out millions of unsolicited Easter Seals in the hope that recipients will feel obligated to make a gift at least in repayment. This is a shoddy practice, frowned on by ethical fund raisers, and extremely expensive to conduct. It is nearly impossible to calculate exactly how much of each dollar contributed goes to fund raising, because this society's financial reports have such broad categories as "Public Information" and "Education," as well as the usual "Administration" and "Fund Raising." My rough estimate of the true expense connected with each dollar given by the public in the annual compaign is around $.40. Quite apart from that, despite the heart-rending pictures of the brace-weighted child, about 40 percent of the money expended on services to children is for "Speech, Hearing, and Related Disorders," as compared to about 10 percent spent for "orthopedic disabilities." While we can easily understand that a photograph of a child with his hand cupped to his ear to assist him in hearing would have less fund-raising appeal than the crippled waifs we are customarily shown, such an image would be more honest advertising in view of this agency's allocations.

The American Lung Association — which, formed in 1904 to combat tuberculosis, was the country's first voluntary health association — also uses seals to raise funds. Mailing the Christmas Seals to about 50 million people each year costs the Association approximately $10 million annually, and the solicitation raises around $35 million. Following the example of other organizations that changed focus once the diseases they were founded to fight had been conquered (new, active cases of tuberculosis were down to fewer than 33,000 in 1972), the American Lung Association now addresses itself to other respiratory diseases.

When we shift from our study of individual agencies to survey the entire contribution made by the voluntary health agencies, we are forced to admit that their role is minor. In 1973, the thirty-six largest voluntary agencies spent $457 million (see Appendix B1, p. 172). We know that anywhere from 15 to 20 percent of these expenditures went toward fund raising and administration. In the same period, federal, state, and local governments were estimated as spending over $37 billion on various aspects of health care.

While the health agencies are very junior partners to government, they are nevertheless partners. The voluntary agencies cooperate to varying degrees with their corresponding federal, state, and local bureaus. Historically, this was not always true. When government first entered the various research areas that had hitherto been the sole province of the philanthropic agencies, there was resentment at the intrusion. But the fact that voluntary efforts were inadequate to meet the challenge was so obvious to the public that gradually most of the hostility to governmental efforts subsided and an arm's-length partnership was established. Today, at the very least, all of the health agencies cooperate with government by testifying before legislative bodies, offering the services of their expert witnesses at government-sponsored forums, and in many cases maintaining Washington representatives willing to assist in the ever-recurring struggle to secure adequate funds. All nineteen of the voluntary agencies that are members of the National Health Council report that they maintain liaison with those governmental agencies working in the same field. Several report legislative cooperation with the appropriate National Institute of Health within their field. At least one, the National Heart Association, takes pride in the fact that its leaders played a major role in bringing about the foundation of the National Heart Institute in

1948. Of the nineteen voluntary agencies, all but five receive grants from federal agencies; and three of these five agencies do accept contracts to perform specific work for the government. Twelve member agencies accept grants on either an occasional or, in two cases, a sustaining basis. Two other agencies act as fiscal agents for governmental expenditures for specific programs. The overall picture that emerges is that government administrators are prepared to utilize the machinery established by voluntary agencies when the agencies are willing and when the establishment of duplicate machinery would be obviously wasteful or inefficient.

In view of the repeated though unaccepted recommendations for consolidation and reform, and the relatively small financial contribution made by the health agencies as compared to government, we are entitled to ask whether our society is well served by their continued activity. Should not the government, in view of its already overwhelming participation, do the whole job? The agencies make one contribution, which we have not yet considered, that I believe dictates a negative response to that question.

This key factor is the energy, time, effort, and education of the millions of volunteers who participate in the activities of the philanthropic health agencies. When the orderly processes of government assume responsibility for a program, be it the erection of dams or the waging of war, the private citizen is apt to shrug his shoulders, conclude that the program is in the good hands of experts, and, until a major scandal emerges, turn his back on governmental processes unless his private interests are directly affected.

But when citizens voluntarily participate in a program, their enthusiasm can be maintained only by providing them with a sense of responsibility for its success or failure. We have already seen that much of the volunteer initiative in the health agencies is provided by the visitation of some ailment, often fatal, on relatives or friends of the recruit. Once the initial step of joining the volunteer army has been taken, the continuity of interest depends on the emotional rewards to the volunteer. The ranks of this army are composed of America's economic elite, for those who have steady jobs cannot afford to devote time to the voluntary health cause. We are, therefore, inspecting upper-middle-class or upper-class citizens when we review the ranks of the voluntary legions. These same people may donate funds to their political party's candidate at election time, but they do not take the same intense interest in bureaucratic processes that they lavish on the work of their favorite philanthropic agency. This interest may be measured in terms of money; namely, the amount each agency's volunteers donate or raise for their favorite cause. But quite apart from this concrete measurement, the volunteers' contributions consist in the information they gather and in turn disseminate; their knowledge, be it only pseudoscientific, of the health problems under attack; and their success in proselytizing additional recruits. The volunteers' services are invaluable, because the devotion that prompts them is not purchasable. That some of these efforts are misguided, that some of this energy could be better expended elsewhere is obvious. But any casual reader of the daily newspapers is well aware that governmentally conducted programs are a long way from 100 percent efficient.

The magnitude of the volunteer effort becomes clear when we examine the numbers of volunteers working for fourteen of the larger agencies.

Agency	Number of Volunteers
American Cancer Society	2,300,000
American Diabetes Association	15,000
American Heart Association	2,000,000
Arthritis Foundation	430,000
National Association for Mental Health	1,000,000
National Association for Retarded Children	130,000
National Cystic Fibrosis	300,000
National Easter Seal Society for Crippled Children and Adults	800,000
National Hemophilia Foundation	230,000
Muscular Dystrophy Association	1,500,000
Multiple Sclerosis Society	500,000
American Lung Association	200,000
United Cerebral Palsy Association	50,000
National Foundation (March of Dimes)	2,000,000

Clearly, these estimates (furnished by the agencies) cannot possibly reflect the degree of involvement of these millions of people. Many work for only one week a year during the annual fund-raising campaign. Others devote half time to the work, and doubtless there are still others on a regular full-time schedule.

Whether the cures for any of these diseases would be delayed if these armies were disbanded is debatable. However, there is no question that much would be lost in terms of public health information, political pressures on government to grant appropriations for research, and enthusiasm and support for the scientists toiling in their laboratories to advance knowledge. Much as funerals are really conducted for the living, since the dead are beyond caring, the health agencies may be said to offer greater benefits to the unafflicted than they do to the diseased.

CHAPTER 11

The Starving Arts

HISTORICALLY, THE ARTS have been encouraged by an admixture of government subsidy and the contributions of wealthy patrons. Over the centuries, the proportions of aid furnished from these two sources has varied greatly, and even in America today the admixture is in a state of flux. Whether we consider the early Church a munificent patron or a branch of government, which it certainly was, the treasures of the Renaissance were sponsored, commissioned, and nurtured in large part from this source.

When we examine support for our present cultural institutions, we must separate the collections of artistic production from contemporary creative effort. While the financial problems of libraries, museums, zoos, and botanical gardens are as massive as those faced by the performing arts, the government, reacting to public pressures, has been far more responsive to maintaining the collections as opposed to encouraging the creators. Libraries, of course, exemplify the closest approach to necessity of any of the collections. Quite apart from their recreational functions, libraries are essential for education and research. Thus, most of the country's nearly 7000 public libraries have almost completely passed through the transition from philanthropic to total government support. Local libraries in smaller communities sometimes solicit philanthropic funds to finance expanded buildings and of course most will accept gifts of valuable book collections. In addition to municipal and state aid received in 1973, libraries were allocated $140 million by the federal government. This amounted to less than 5 percent of the total budget of the 12,000 public and educational libraries in the country, and there is no assurance this aid will continue.

An exception to the pattern of government support exists at one of the country's greatest collections, the New York Public Library. The financial problems faced by this institution arise both because of its philanthropic heritage and its misleading name. The truth is that the New York Public really consists of two library systems. One is the Circulation Department, made up of some 85 branch libraries; this service to all boroughs of the city is supported by public funds allocated by the city. The other — and from the scholar's and researcher's point of view the more valuable — part is the Research Department, housed in the stone lion-guarded, two-block-long structure on Fifth Avenue. This priceless collection, safeguarded in its massive fireproof building, originated in philanthropic donations by John Jacob Astor, James Lenox, Samuel Tilden, Andrew Carnegie, Payne Whitney, and others. Until present times the income from endowments, contributions, and foundation grants have added to and maintained this collection of nearly 4 million books, 9 million manuscripts, 126,000 prints, and 290,000 maps. But in 1970–71, the trustees faced a deficit of nearly $2 million even though the state of New York had granted $2.3 million in aid from its Council on the Arts. As a result of the unbalanced budget, the Research Department reduced the hours it was open to the public from eighty-seven to seventy-two a week.[1]

In addition to this plight of the New York Public, many private libraries that are open on a membership basis and many private college libraries have serious financial problems. However, speaking generally, it is clear that the popular demand throughout the country for publicly supported, easily accessible, local libraries indicates that the pressure on government to relieve philanthropy will continue.

The nation's more than 500 art museums, founded and, until recently, maintained entirely by philanthropy, are also facing financial problems that are forcing them to seek government aid. In many ways these museums are victims of their own popularity. Across the country in the last decade, museum attendance has increased at an accelerating rate. As a result, most have needed more professional personnel, guards, and attendants than ever before. Museum employees in a number of cities have joined unions, and wages have risen sharply. Acquisition costs for new works have increased greatly, as the general inflationary spiral has transformed objects of art into an excellent financial investment for the private collector.

While most museums charge an admission fee, many admit schoolchildren and organized student groups without charge. New York's Museum of Modern Art recently raised its admission fee to $2, but its deficits will continue. As a result of the economic squeeze, many museums are using such large segments of their endowment funds that these reserves are threatened with early extinction. The New York State Council on the Arts recently estimated that most museums in the state would exhaust their total endowments within twelve years, with the Museum of Modern Art's disappearing within five years and the Whitney Museum's within six to eight.

Quite apart from soaring operating costs, museums find themselves short of gallery exhibition space as a result of gifts of priceless pictures and in some cases of total collections. When the Lehman Collection, consisting of over 3000 European objects of art estimated to be worth approximately $100 million, was bequeathed to the Metropolitan in 1969, it was stipulated that the collection was to be preserved "forever" as a separate entity within the Museum. Unquestionably, funds for the erection of suitable facilities to house this collection must come from voluntary donations. Leaving valuable collections to museums is greatly encouraged by our present inheritance tax laws. As one lawyer said of the Lehman gift, "For anyone with a collection like that, leaving it to a museum is the only sensible thing to do."[2] It is clear that as more rich collectors die the irreplaceable objects will more and more find their way into the country's museums, requiring more gallery space, attracting more visitors, and requiring more personnel.

Nor are major art museums the only collections of work of great value presently facing inexorable financial pressure. In New York City alone there are at least seventy-nine museums exhibiting different aspects of our physical and cultural heritage. In nearly every city and major town in the country, objects of at least local interest are on display, and in many cases the exhibitions are of far wider than local interest. Monticello, Mount Vernon, the Lee House, and a thousand other former residences of the great or near great around the country house material of major value to scholars and of considerable interest even to casual visitors. Nearly all these repositories, whether natural history museums, archeological exhibits, or historical collections, are understaffed, or the staffs are underpaid. Collections that should be open to public view are closed for lack of supervision, or hours are so limited as to deny maximum accessibility. The curator of the Smithsonian Institution, in a beautifully written series of essays on museums, concludes:

> Museums are hideously understaffed and underfinanced today. They cannot possibly cope with increasing demands placed upon them by everyone, from the public to the school system to scholars . . . Either the museums will fold and close their doors, like the poor old mistreated railroads, or someone will have sense enough to realize that real education is fun, and that the museums' sort of education has to be paid for, just like all the other kinds.[3]

America's more than 100 zoos have much the same history as her museums. Many were founded by individuals or zoological societies formed by private citizens, but as attendance increased, municipalities took over much of the financial responsibility and in some cases the actual administration. Currently the typical situation is one in which philanthropic donations partly finance new facilities while admissions and municipal subsidies keep operating deficits at a manageable level. With the gradual contraction of our wilderness areas where wildlife can thrive and with heightened public interest in all phases of conservation, zoo attendance has risen to new highs in most cities.

Botanical gardens do not seem beset by quite so serious financial problems as other types of collections. Those gardens attached to universities to furnish material for study and research in botany share the problems of their parent institutions. However, many of the finest gardens have resulted from bequests, and endowments for maintenance almost always accompanied the gift of land. Modest admission charges and membership dues assist those gardens for which maintenance costs have outstripped endowment income.

A survey of all the collections except libraries, conducted by the National Council on the Arts for the fiscal year 1972–73, disclosed that of the $513 million income received during that period by 1821 art and history museums, zoos, gardens, and aquariums, 63 percent came from philanthropy and 37 percent from government. The attendance by the public at all these museums was more than 308 million. Nearly 50,000 professional employees served these collections and 64,000 volunteers donated full- or part-time service.[4]

Public interest diminishes and attendance is far lower for the performing arts; consequently, political pressures for government subsidy in this area are correlatively less than those exerted to sustain libraries, museums, and other collections. With the exception of the Depression's WPA program, which was more a relief measure than a subsidy of the arts, the federal government did not appropriate major funds to encourage the arts until 1965. In that year, President Johnson signed a bill creating the National Foundation for the Arts and Humanities, a concept that had originated in President Kennedy's administration. In less than ten years the appropriation for this fund has reached the vicinity of $70 million annually. Although this total equates to about $.30 per citizen, England appropriates $1.23, Canada $1.40, and West Germany $2.42 to assist corresponding programs.[5] However, such comparisons with other countries are not entirely relevant to our situation. Through the device of the tax-exempt gift, the United States does encourage the arts to the extent that gifts are made in this direction.

Major government subsidy in the near future is unlikely, because the political philosophy of most American legislators is that general tax funds should be used solely for the general benefit of all taxpayers. Cultural institutions are not necessary to survival; they only enrich our lives once survival is assured. Furthermore, rather small segments of the population take advantage of any one facet of their cultural opportunities. Compared to the population as a whole, the audience for symphonies, the dance, or even the legitimate theater is relatively small and apt to be the best educated and most affluent segment of our society — the segment most able to pay for its cultural needs, at least in the minds of legislators. This philosophy is hard to counter except with appeals to national pride — along lines that American dance should be at

least as good as Russian or that our opera should attain the
high quality of its Italian counterpart. Appeals of this
kind, however, are more persuasive to Congress when
applied to our space effort, our scientific achievements, or
our health programs.

There is another argument against direct government
subsidy, at least to the creative artist, that is heard both
from legislators and from some artists. This argument
warns of the deleterious effect of political influence being
exerted in a field where the freedom to create must remain
unhampered. Senator Proxmire, for example, during a
debate on the size of appropriations for subsidies of the
arts warned against the "dead hand of government." The
flaw in this argument — namely, that when government
did subsidize artists in the WPA program, the work remained free of political influence — fails to still this line
of opposition.

Most of the states and even some territories have created
arts agencies to grant support funds. Appropriations,
which started modestly, grew to $8 million by 1970 and
have increased substantially each year since. It is hardly
surprising that New York, with its many cultural activities centered in New York City, led in the size of appropriations. Nearly $15 million was appropriated in 1973,
the last year of Governor Rockefeller's administration, and
his successor, Governor Wilson, appealed for a $30 million
appropriation for 1974–75.[6] Of more magnitude in total
is the financial assistance rendered by certain municipalities, prompted by civic pride in the orchestra, opera company, or repertory theater offered in their performing arts
centers. But despite government's growing role, not even

the most optimistic prediction would envisage the transition from philanthropy to government support that we have witnessed in the fields of health, education, and child care.

The economic problems of symphony orchestras exemplify the financial plight common to the performing arts. In 1967, the presidents of 90 principal orchestras attended a conference in New York's Philharmonic Hall. These men discussed the problems of some 1400 different organizations, of which only 54 were composed predominantly of professional musicians, located in virtually every city with a population of over 50,000 in the country. Some 20 million people attend over 11,000 concerts a year. Musicians in these orchestras teach music to students at all levels as well as organize concerts of chamber music and other forms. Years ago, these orchestras limited themselves almost exclusively to subscription concerts, but today 70 percent of their activities consist of such public services as concerts for children and the general public in parks and on tours. The ninety orchestra presidents prepared the following unhappy figures, which they presented to a congressional appropriations committee.

90 Principal American Orchestras

Year	Total Expenses	Cash Loss
1963	$28,820,500	$ 169,800
1969	66,794,500	5,215,800
1972 (estimated)	87,090,000	13,222,000

The largest part of orchestra expense is the compensation to the musicians. As in much other philanthropic work, the employees historically were partial contributors

to the project by reason of the low wages they were forced
to accept. As a result of the depressed levels of the past,
these wages are slated to take larger percentage increases
than those of industrial employees and even then will not
be comparable. Unionization of orchestra musicians has
been spreading in recent years, and New York's Philharmonic has faced several crippling strikes of long duration.
The conference estimated that, while expenses in 1972
would be up by 30 percent over 1969 to $87 million,
income would increase only about 20 percent, or $40 mil-
lion, because any further raise in the prices of tickets and
subscriptions would so limit attendance that the very purpose for which the orchestras exist would be frustrated.
According to the estimate, contributions would also rise
by 20 percent, to $33 million, still leaving a cash loss of
over $13 million. As in all other situations in which
philanthropy fails to meet needs, those responsible for the
budgets are seeking government subsidy to erase the red
ink. The specific request to government was to meet 10
percent of gross costs — at the time, some $8.5 million for
those orchestras that qualified by maintaining a high level
of both audience and contributor support, being efficiently
managed, and conducting broad-based programs for the
general public. In the years following, government subsidy never reached more than 5 percent. Without substantial help, an increasing number of orchestras will be
silenced, yet government intervention to the degree requested would appear to be only a remote probability.[7]

Philanthropic support of symphonies originally came
almost exclusively from major donors. Henry L. Higgin-
son of Boston set the pattern in 1881 when he proclaimed

his resolve "to hire an orchestra of sixty men and a conductor, paying them all by the year." He anticipated a deficit of $50,000, for which $1 million in principal was needed, and he personally provided that amount.[8] In the following decades, rich men in Chicago, New York, Philadelphia, and other major cities donated the funds to establish orchestras. Today the gifts of large individual donors, who have not disappeared entirely, are being supplemented by a mounting total of contributions from an increasing number of individuals; over 85 percent of the total number of contributions made to symphony orchestras are in amounts of less than $100. But the totals thus raised are inadequate.

The closing of the seventy-four-year-old Dallas Symphony Orchestra illustrates the plight these organizations currently face. With a population of under a million, Dallas boasts nearly 4000 individuals with annual incomes over $50,000 and 400 millionaires. Despite the wealth of the community, a public fund-raising campaign achieved a measly $30,000. All gifts together failed to meet the matching conditions of the Ford Foundation's $2 million grant, and in late 1974, unable to pay the musicians, the orchestra suspended operations.[9]

Opera's economic problems are even more difficult to solve. Opera is more expensive to produce, has a smaller potential audience, and attracts an insufficient number of financial supporters. Four major opera companies exist in the United States: New York's Metropolitan, the New York City Opera, the Chicago Lyric, and the San Francisco Opera. There are, in addition, about forty professional opera companies that produce fewer than twenty-five performances a year each. The more ambitious the programs of any opera company, the larger are its deficits and the more acute its financial problems.

The largest, New York's Metropolitan, encountered difficulty from its very inception. In 1883, the first season, it lost $600,000, which caused the ouster of the initial management. In the Depression year 1932, the Met announced it would not present a season because of insufficient funds. A "tin cup" campaign, instituted by Mrs. August Belmont, resulted in survival funds. In 1953, a performance of *Tristan und Isolde* was purposely interrupted to dramatize the company's dire need. But by all odds the most serious problems were raised in 1966 when the Met abandoned its baroque home and moved to Lincoln Center. Today, the huge house can produce $45,000 for each performance with attendance at 90 percent of capacity, but the cost of the lavish productions averages $75,000 each. "We lose $30,000 just by raising the curtain," says the Assistant General Manager. Housekeeping expenses and spiraling wages for performers and musicians alike add to the problems. In 1972, the operating deficit was $7.8 million, compared to five years earlier when there was a $3.5 million loss. But in the earlier year, contributions offset the deficit, whereas in 1972 there was a $2.8 million gap.[10] The anticipated deficit for 1974 is $6 million. As a result, the Metropolitan has announced a reduction of four to six weeks in its 1975 schedule of performances.[11] The price scale for tickets has increased steadily over the years; currently, orchestra tickets sell at $17.50. Even so, subscribers have been asked to contribute voluntarily 20 percent more than the price of their tickets, and over half have sent contributions of varying amounts.[12] In the pattern common to all philanthropies unable to raise sufficient funds, the Met is now trying to obtain government support, but not even the most hopeful believe that aid from this source will be a permanent solution. The state responded through its Council on the Arts by grants of $328,000 in 1969, $200,000 in 1970, and around the same amount in succeeding years. The National Endowment for the Arts granted $1 million in matching funds for 1974–75.[13] The problems faced by other opera companies are similar, and if their plight is less acute, it is only because their programs are on a less costly scale.

The relatively few dance companies that have any claim to professionalism and permanency face a less severe economic problem because productions are not as costly to mount. The Ford Foundation made a large grant to encourage ballet nationally, and at least in the case of the New York City Ballet both state and city have given aid. Despite assistance from private and public funds, ballet and other dance companies have curtailed programs and in several recent instances have been forced out of existence.

Accurate information as to the total given to support the arts is not obtainable. A fair guess would put the aggregate somewhat under $1 billion annually, of which 75 percent is donated by individuals, 15 percent by foundations, and the remainder by corporations and government subsidy. In addition, United Arts Funds have been established in a number of communities to form an easy method of contributing to a wide range of cultural projects. St. Paul, Winston-Salem, Cincinnati, and Dallas all instituted joint funds of this kind during the 1960s.

Despite the ascending philanthropic aid to the arts in recent years, far greater sums will be needed in the future. In 1974 the Ford Foundation, in a massive study projecting the future for the performing arts, made the gloomy prediction that by 1981 over $300 million would be required from philanthropy to bridge the deficit gap as compared to about $60 million today.[14] Support of the arts is one area in which we can safely predict that government will never play more than a secondary role. If our arts are to be encouraged as they should be, philanthropy will have to play not only a larger but a more imaginative and innovative role. In manufacturing, productivity can increase through the use of machines, computers, and all kinds of technological advances. Expenses are kept in line as productivity improves, so that cost per unit is held within the reach of purchasers. But there is no way productivity can increase in the arts. More books require more library shelves; more pictures need additional gallery space and a larger guard force. The number of dancers in a ballet, the number of musicians in an orchestra, the number of actors in *Hamlet* cannot be reduced regardless of economic pressures. While other services may achieve expense reduction, the costs of cultural collections or performances will inevitably increase.

CHAPTER 12

Education's Insatiable Needs

TOTAL ANNUAL EXPENDITURES for all educational processes
in the United States are estimated at around $90 billion.[1]
Municipal and state governments shoulder the greatest
part of the burden, with the federal government assuming
an estimated $8.5 billion as subsidiary aid. Philan-
thropy's share is around 4 percent of the total, or $3.9
billion in 1973.[2] Omitting from this discussion institutions supported in whole or in part by religious organizations, it is generally believed that about two thirds of
philanthropy's contribution goes to colleges and universities and one-third to secondary and elementary schools.

Ever since the public school system emerged, debate has
raged over whether the private schools serve the best interests of what most people like to think of as our equalitarian
society. There is no doubt that the private schools, for the
most part, serve the interests of the middle class — particularly the upper middle class and the rich. The private
schools and colleges take pride in the fact that they produce more leaders, more corporate heads, more profes-

sional men, and more people listed in *Who's Who* than their proportionate share of the population. On the other hand, their critics contend that they produce an elitist, snobbish upper class that considers itself superior and is afforded opportunities not open to those who attend less prestigious schools.

All major cities and nearly all affluent suburbs have private schools from nursery school straight through the high school level. For the most part, these exclusive institutions finance themselves by high tuitions and a smattering of gifts from parents and alumni. Many of these schools offer a few scholarships to children whose parents cannot afford the high stipend, but nearly all the children of the lower middle class receive their early training in the public schools. The private schools conduct fund drives, particularly to finance new construction and scholarship funds.

According to a survey conducted by the *New York Times* in 1968–69, some 26,000 pupils, or less than 2 percent of all students, attended private day schools in New York City. This total may be slightly higher than the percentage for the typical American city, as the public school crisis in New York has encouraged many parents who can afford it to send their children to one of the private schools. Between 1960 and 1969, expanded private school facilities in the city permitted an increase of approximately 4500 students, or about 20 percent. Perhaps 1000 private school pupils in the city are black children, most of whom are attending on scholarships. In 1969, the private schools had a total scholarship fund of about $2.8 million. There are about 2000 teachers in New York's private schools, as compared with 59,000 in the public school system, but though tuitions range to above $2000 per year, the salaries for private school teachers are considerably lower than the scales won by the teachers' union in the public school system. There seems to be no argument that, with the exception of a few outstanding public schools, the private schools afford students a superior education. More than 95 percent of those who wish to continue on to college do so. The smaller classes, the higher degree of discipline, and the availability of individual instruction explain the superior results over those achieved by the strife-torn city school system.[3]

Leaving the day schools and viewing the boarding schools as a group, we see a larger role played by philanthropy. Criticism of the boarding school has been raised almost from its establishment. As early as 1902, George C. Edwards wrote in the *Educational Review*, "The worst of boarding schools are ineffectual reformatories, and the best of them are scrupulously cultivated hotbeds of snobbishness and un-American class superiority . . . [The] fact is that these costly boarding schools are in reality but a species of orphan asylum — only without the claim on our sympathies that legitimate asylums have. The parents are not dead, but selfish."[4]

At the present time the boarding schools are in trouble, both with respect to receiving financial support and because of stable or declining enrollment. In early 1971, the National Association of Independent Schools, which has some 800 member institutions, reported that enrollment in military schools had dropped greatly because of the unpopularity of the war in Vietnam. Lesser declines have occurred over the years in boarding schools that are not co-educational.[5] Two other factors also contribute to the enrollment decline. First, the boarding schools' tuitions are becoming so high that only the rich can still pay them. In addition, more children of the rich are unwilling to give up the comforts of home life for the more rigorous regimens and the more monastic life of boarding schools.

The decline in enrollment spells serious financial trouble ahead, because expenses are met largely by tuition, which contributes up to 84.6 percent at girls' day schools and 76.5 percent at boys' boarding schools. The decline is caused by the fact that colleges have broadened their scope of admissions to include more poor students and more representatives from minorities, and therefore prep school training is no longer an automatic admission ticket to first-rate colleges. Many of the boys' prep schools have sought to meet the enrollment crisis by accepting girls as well as more day students.

There are perhaps 3000 boarding schools in the country, of which 200 participate in the Secondary School Admission Tests program, but when boarding schools are mentioned, most people think of the less than 100 schools centered in New England. Some of these, the oldest (for example, Andover, Exeter, St. Paul's, Groton, Choate), have endowments funds, but many of the newer ones are not so fortunate.

Higher education attracts perhaps $2 billion a year in gifts, of which 85 percent goes to the private colleges and the remaining 15 percent to some of the great state universities, particularly in those states that do not contain major private institutions. While all recipients would prefer to receive unrestricted funds, special purpose gifts are highly acceptable, and education presents a wide variety of choices to the donor. Scholarships that directly benefit worthy students who cannot afford tuition do not directly aid the universities, although they permit a selection of a greater admixture of students. The endowment of a faculty chair memorializes the donor and defrays faculty costs. However, this is only true when an existing professorship is endowed, for if a new department or course is involved, establishing the supporting research, laboratories, and teaching material would involve costs beyond the salary of one professor. Capital gifts for the new construction of desirable facilities are often sought in major fund-raising campaigns, but overall costs are frequently raised rather than lowered by the acceptance of gifts for new buildings. Gifts of art or valuable book collections present another choice to donors. Yet despite the annually increasing sum of gifts, higher education faces serious financial problems.

The rising deficits have two major causes. The first is that, as in many other personal service institutions, increased productivity has not accompanied inflationary costs. Secondly, the American system of higher education is increasingly viewed as wasteful of time and money by observers, and irrelevant by students. Perhaps at no time in our history have such jaundiced looks been focused on the universities by such a diversity of critics. Few other institutions facing financial crisis would permit their expensive physical facilities to remain virtually unused and unproductive for nearly one third of the year. By compressing the long vacation periods, students could complete courses in far less time. Perhaps the removal of so many young people from the roster of job-seekers for the additional year is beneficial to the unemployment problem, but it would seem that we should be able to find fruitful occupations for those presently occupied in unnecessarily extended periods of study.

In 1970, the concern over the plight of universities reached a high point. In a study conducted in that year by the Carnegie Commission of Higher Education (headed by Dr. Clark Kerr, former head of the University of California) of forty-one private and public colleges and universities in twenty-one states, 70 percent were found to be either in financial straits or "headed for trouble." The list included some of the wealthiest institutions in the country, even Harvard with its endowment funds of over $1 billion.

In addition to this survey, individual news stories confirmed and indeed amplified the findings. "NYU Loss Put at $4.5 Million, 3 Times More Than Last Year's" — so read the *New York Times* at the end of 1970.[6] "Princeton Plans to Cut Staff and Raise Tuition to Reduce Deficit" read the headline over a story concerning the University's $2.5 million deficit for the fiscal year 1970–71.[7] Columbia announced a $15 million budget deficit for the same year.[8] The cries of pain from the smaller colleges do not attract such large headlines, but they are just as loud if not louder.

Despite inflation and other adverse factors, including declining attendance, by 1973 most of the institutions studied by the Carnegie Commission had improved their conditions. By reducing services and raising tuitions, a number of universities which had earlier reported trouble indicated improvement. Since 1968, tuitions of public institutions have been rising at about 7 percent a year and those of private colleges have gone up by about 8 percent. In 1968, private tuitions were $1000 greater than public tuitions, but in 1973 the gap had widened to $1500. With a declining number of students seeking admission, the private colleges were in an increasingly difficult competitive position.

Authorities agree that the private universities must continue to exist and set high standards as well as save taxpayers uncounted millions. But like so many other areas in which the financial problems are beyond philanthropy's capacity, pressure will be put on government to assist. Undoubtedly, the most politically feasible method of support would be to make state or federal grants available for low- and middle-income students in order to offset the difference in tuition between public and private colleges. Even in the event of such a development, philanthropy would still have to continue its effort in this area.[9]

While all private colleges are facing difficult problems, the Negro colleges in the South are confronted with near disaster. There are 128 predominantly Negro colleges with an enrollment of some 130,000 students. Roughly three quarters of these schools are privately financed. In 1970, the federal government offered $20 million in special funds for construction loans, with the proviso that the colleges would have to raise $1 for every $3 the government contributed. The colleges were so poor that only $4 million of the matching funds were used within the year. These schools cannot charge much for tuition because their students cannot afford to pay much; in 1968, 63 percent of the freshmen at these colleges came from families with annual incomes of less than $6000. The alumni are not rich and endowments are virtually non-existent. The United Negro College Fund, a money-raising organization for 41 of the colleges, raised only $10.5 million in 1973. The largest total the organization ever raised, since its founding in 1944, was $11.4 million in 1971. Even this represented only a small part of the very inadequate $110 million total that these colleges spent on 40,000 students.

Faculty salary levels at the Negro colleges are one-half the national average; the standard salary is $6800 a year. The northern universities, ever on the alert for a chance to integrate their faculties, raid the southern schools for the best teachers, and incidentally, in their drive for a larger black enrollment, for the most promising students as well.

The Carnegie Commission on Higher Education released a report on the Negro colleges in 1971 making detailed recommendations to improve their critical situation, but the nub of the report indicated that if its recommendations were accepted the black colleges would require $356 million in federal aid instead of the approximately $120 million they were then receiving.[10] In addition, private philanthropy would have to raise substantially more than it had to date if the Negro colleges were to catch up with other educational institutions and expand to handle the future's enlarged enrollment.

When we examine postgraduate education and the professional schools operated by the major universities, we find no less clamor for philanthropic funds. Many universities have fund-raising policies for these separate subdivisions such that each is responsible for raising its own funds, or "each tub rests on its own bottom." One of the troubles with this philosophy is that some of the less important schools academically — schools of business administration, for example — have relatively little trouble raising money because of the interest of the corporate community. In contrast, segments of the university that are more important from an academic viewpoint — such as divinity schools or schools of dentistry — have considerable difficulty raising funds.

The professional schools currently attracting the greatest public attention because of personnel shortages and inflationary costs are the medical schools. There are currently not enough doctors or dentists or paramedical personnel, and under the present rate of training, the shortage will continue and become more acute in the future. The Carnegie Commission on Higher Education studied the medical school problem and released its report in late 1970.[11] It recommended an expansion of present medical schools to accommodate 39 to 44 percent more entrants and the creation of at least nine new schools, which would add 1350 entrant places. As each new medical school costs somewhere over $100 million to start and the education of a single student can run as high as $16,000 a year, it is obvious that government will have to play the major role in expanding medical training to meet society's needs. However, a reverse trend is occurring: there has been a reduction in federal research grants, which are essential to maintaining faculties of high quality.

Education's financial demands are insatiable. It has proven possible to reduce deficits by cutting services, eliminating research programs, increasing class sizes, and accepting fewer students unable to pay the high tuitions, but these economies inevitably result in a lowering of standards. Philanthropy is not massive enough to reverse this trend, but the maintenance of our private educational institutions at every level should receive the highest donor priority.

CHAPTER 13

Racial Minorities –
The Struggle for Equality

SINCE THE MID-NINETEENTH CENTURY when antislavery citizens organized to abolish human bondage, philanthropic groups have formed and multiplied to aid in the solution of the nearly insolvable problems of racial minorities. The major effort has always been focused on the relationship between blacks and the white majority, but voluntary groups have countered discrimination against other minorities, including Jews, Indians, Puerto Ricans, and Mexican, Japanese, and Chinese Americans. Although some of these organizations have existed for decades, the problems they were formed to combat have not disappeared; indeed, despite some progress, major racial tension has become more acute rather than less with the passage of time. Paradoxically, the very progress which has been achieved so painstakingly at such cost of money and energy has heightened the intensity of the problem by raising hopes, always unfulfilled, of equal justice and an end to discrimination. Only the Jews, who are relatively difficult to distinguish physically from the majority, have made what could be considered satisfactory progress in combating discrimination, and even in their case the struggle is by no means ended. Where complexion makes distinction easy, the problems so far surpass the solutions that even the victims cannot agree on what policies present the best hopes for alleviation.

The oldest and in many ways still the most effective antidiscrimination group is the NAACP. This organization's policy from its very inception in 1909 has been to improve the lot of the Negro until he becomes entirely integrated into American society. The goals are for black children to learn together with whites, to grow up and work together, to live in the same communities, and to have the same opportunities. The NAACP has rejected violence as a tactic and is at odds with the militant segments of the black community that espouse violence and separatism. The NAACP's long-time Executive Director, Roy Wilkins, has stated, "We firmly and forthrightly reject violence, race hate and related tactics. We continue to seek an integrated America where white and black men and women can live, work and learn side by side. Any other approach is suicidal for America and for the Negro people."

The NAACP's history and record of accomplishment has been described at length.[1] Currently, this organization has over 1300 branches, a paid membership of over 350,000 people, and an annual income of nearly $4 million. Both membership and income have declined slightly in recent years. Because the NAACP openly lobbies and makes every effort to affect legislation favorable to minorities, gifts to it are not tax-exempt. However, a closely allied organization, the NAACP Legal Defense and Educational Fund, which furnishes scholarships for Negro students and provides legal assistance for those requiring this form of aid, does have tax exemption. Income for this organization approaches $3 million a year.

Created in 1910 only one year after the NAACP's birth, the National Urban League has striven to broaden the employment base for Negroes by cooperating with white employers to furnish qualified personnel for work in every phase of the American economy. In addition to its support for an integrated school system, the League's objectives are to: "Make a planned effort to place qualified Negroes in all categories of employment at all levels of responsibility. Intensify training and apprenticeship programs to prepare new Negro employees and upgrade those already employed." The League's income from donations is around $5 million annually. In addition, during the late 1960s the League received a government grant of over $9 million to provide for coordination of on-the-job training programs. The League has ninety-three local affiliates operating through five regional offices. As the League's program is based on cooperation with white industry and white labor leaders, approximately half its trustees are white. Both the NAACP and the Urban League are considered stodgy and "Uncle Tom" by the more aggressive and youthful black organizations, which believe that more militant methods than those espoused by either of the older organizations would hasten the achievement of black goals.

A third and much more recent organization, the Urban Coalition, was created even while the smoke from racial riots hung over the streets of Detroit and Newark in 1967. The horror and attendant fear spawned by the race riots, looting, and violence in a dozen cities furnished the impetus for the hasty formation of this new movement. The concept was that the self-interest of great corporations should dictate a massive injection of corporate know-how as well as money to rectify the problems which fostered the unrest. Their enthusiasm goaded by a determination that society not be allowed to tear itself apart in fratricide, the formulators of the Urban Coalition promulgated a most ambitious outline for a reform program. Individuals as well as foundations and corporations were solicited to contribute for such wide objectives as improved housing, better education, job training, and even the capitalizing of small business ventures, which hopefully would employ increasing numbers of blacks. Even though some $6 million was raised by the Coalition and its sister organization, Urban America, in 1968, the scope of its ambitious plans was severely limited by lack of response from donors. As the streets quieted down, the fears of corporate executives were lulled; contributions, which would have had to be in the scores of millions of dollars to encompass the program, were well under $10 million. Hampered by inadequate support, the Urban Coalition's development was accompanied by general disappointment, which obscured some of the credit it deserved for instituting productive programs. Furthermore, as this disappointment was translated into smaller annual contributions by corporations, programs that showed more promise than concrete results were discontinued. The Coalition's successes were limited by two factors: first, inadequate support for grandiose plans; and second, the fact that the black community had only a small part in planning the programs that white corporate executives thought would effect the most immediate remedies. The result was summarized by the newspaper headline, "Once-Thriving Urban Coalition, Short of Funds, Pares Its Staff."[2]

The experience of the Urban Coalition illustrates the dilemma confronting philanthropists wishing to contribute to causes redressing racial injustice. Without white money in large amounts, voluntary effort is doomed; on the other hand, without black leadership and complete acceptance by the black community, white hopes for improvement, no matter how generously funded, cannot succeed. Understandably enough, black leadership tends to be far more militant in advocating programs than even white liberals. Few whites, apart from the radical student left, are eager to furnish guns or explosives to black groups preaching violence. If whites are going to be killed or even suffer a diminution of their power, they can hardly be expected to cooperate in the effort. History records few instances in which a dominant majority willingly surrendered power to an ambitious minority.

One of the most effective of the popular civil-rights organizations in the sixties, owing in large part to the dynamic leadership of its founder, Martin Luther King, Jr., was the Southern Christian Leadership Council. But even this group, which solicited white money and staged some of the most dramatic though non-violent demonstrations in the South, lost its appeal to younger blacks because of its non-violent position. Since King's assassination, the Conference, under weaker leadership, has become more militant — although it continues to espouse non-violence — and white support has diminished.

The splintering of the civil-rights movement in the mid-sixties came about because black leaders could agree neither on objectives nor on methods for achieving them. Only Urban League and NAACP spokesmen have continued to speak with undiminished prestige in the halls of government. The Student Non-Violent Coordinating Committee, the Congress of Racial Equality, and a number of other organizations organized with high hopes have lost their memberships, their support, and their effectiveness.

Philanthropy's role in alleviating America's major social problem is peripheral. Whether we examine illiteracy, illegitimacy, substandard medical care, inhuman housing facilities, soaring crime rates, or any of the other major evils afflicting us, we are forced to admit that our failure to end interracial strife is the key to our malady. Even government, which over the past century has moved slowly in the direction of reform, has had only a small impact on a problem that becomes more serious as the percentage of black citizens continues to rise. It would seem that philanthropy's most useful role is to undertake programs with limited objectives and easily measurable results. Because it is clear that blacks are suspicious of white leadership in their struggle for equality, self-help programs conducted by blacks offer the most fruitful philanthropic opportunities. Greatly increased aid to the Negro colleges in the South and scholarships for black students who are qualified in every way except economically to attend college, medical schools, or other professional institutions offer a hope of future leadership. Programs of this nature could absorb many times the philanthropic funds available and still be inadequate. It seems tragic to people of good will that programs of wider scope are less effective, but even Congress, with all its power, is unable to legislate the brotherhood of man.

The philanthropic efforts of American Jewry to end anti-Semitism have been motivated more by social than by economic discrimination. Representing only 3 percent of the population (as compared to over 10 percent for Negroes), Jews as a whole have moved from the virtual bottom of the economic ladder to near the top in less than a century. The following table indicates annual income for Jews as compared to the total population as of 1970.[3]

Family Income (Annual)	Jews	Total U.S. Population
Under $3000	16%	21%
$3000 to $7000	27%	44%
$7000 to $10,000	24%	16%
$10,000 to $15,000	24%	12%
$15,000+	9%	7%

Despite the Jews' economic advance, perhaps even because of it, anti-Semitism continues to exist in the United States, although none but the most alarmist could see it as a major threat to Jewish hopes. Some major steel, auto, and public utilities companies hire few Jews and have almost none in high executive positions. On the other hand, the important professions of law, medicine, and teaching have a large component of Jewish citizens.

While Hitler's virtual extinction of German Jews horrified the world and demonstrated all too clearly the ultimate result of virulent anti-Semitism, other factors have kept the embers of hatred aglow. The Israeli-Arab conflicts have embittered those whose interests are oriented to the Arab cause, and the oil embargo imposed by the Arabs added some support from inconvenienced motorists. Curiously, anti-Semitism among blacks has risen in the decades following World War II. As victims of racial prejudice themselves, one would think blacks would eschew hatred of others on similar grounds, but there are several factors that fan the sparks of anti-Semitism among blacks, particularly those who are militant. Discussing only New York City, where the concentration of both Jews and blacks is greater than in any other part of the country, we observe that there are many Jewish slum landlords who show faint interest in the welfare of their black tenants. In addition, there are many small Jewish-owned stores in ghetto areas that allegedly gouge their black customers.

Several Jewish agencies exist to combat anti-Semitism. Foremost and perhaps best known is the Anti-Defamation League, which — through the careful research of a network of reporters, mostly volunteer, around the country and the world — keeps tabs on the stirrings of anti-Semitism. The American Jewish Congress and the American Jewish Committee are not content merely to combat anti-Semitism but endorse a broad scope of activities; both organizations, under somewhat different programs, seek to promote pride in Jewish culture and to encourage support of Jewish institutions.

The minority group suffering the greatest hardships and injustice is the oldest, the one supposedly under the

guardianship of the United States government, and therefore the one for which philanthropy does least — namely,
the 600,000 American Indians. Perhaps history offers
some explanation as to why settlers of new lands have
always been so intent on eliminating the natives.
Whether we consider the Australians' treatment of the
aborigines, the New Zealanders' massacres of the Maoris,
the Spanish decimation of the Aztecs in Mexico, or our
own treatment of the Indians, man's inhumanity to man
seems to reach its peak when applied to indigenous
peoples.

The American Indians have the highest infant mortality rate of any group in the country: 32.2 of every 1000
babies born on Indian reservations die during their first
year, compared to 23.7 infant deaths nationally. On some
reservations the rate ranges to 100 deaths per 1000 births —
about twice as high as in the worst Negro ghettos and five
times the white rate. The life expectancy of Indians on
the reservation is forty-four years, compared to sixty-four
nationally; Alaskan Indians on the average die by the age
of thirty-five. Suicide, the second leading cause of death
among Indians, is particularly high among teen-agers —
at three times the national rate. In 1966, more than
16,000 Indian children of school age were not attending
any school. The average educational level for all Indians
under federal supervision is five school years; drop-out
rates are twice the national average.

The most shocking aspect of this human tragedy is that
the government spends millions through its Bureau of
Indian Affairs. On the second largest reservation, Pine

Ridge Reservation in South Dakota, $8040 a year is spent on each Sioux family; yet, because of high costs for administration, medical services, and education, the median income is $1910 per family. While there is one government employee for nearly every family, the unemployment rate among the Indian work force is over 60 percent.[4]

As we would expect in this situation, since government has assumed almost total responsibility for the welfare of a group of citizens, philanthropic effort has diminished nearly to the vanishing point. The Bureau of Indian Affairs, a body within the framework of the Interior Department, is responsible for safeguarding and improving the lot of the nearly 400,000 Indians who live on reservations. The Indians, of course, are free to leave reservations and become assimilated into the rest of American society, and some 200,000 — about one third of the total population — have chosen to give up their ancient tribal cultures for the dubious benefits of our industrialized society. Some have prospered; many others have failed to adjust. But the major problem is posed by the vast majority who steadfastly cling to their remaining tribal lands, their diverse languages, and their traditions. To say that the Bureau of Indian Affairs has, despite its intention, failed to give its wards a better life is understatement.

Nor have voluntary efforts to supplement government activity been either massive or particularly effective. Of the twenty-eight voluntary agencies listed by the Bureau of Indian Affairs as involved in some aspect of helping the Indian, nearly half are supported by various Christian churches and are interested more in bringing Christ to the heathen than in bringing happiness to the red man. Even the two most important agencies are relatively small in size and expenditures. In a recent year the Association on American Indian Affairs, with the general objective of assisting the Indian, spent about $650,000, which it had received from its 45,000 members and other contributors. A number of this agency's thirty-eight board members are Indians. A still smaller agency, Arrow, spent roughly $150,000 in the same year, mainly on job-training programs. Eight Indians form a majority of this agency's twelve-member board. In a few cities with concentrations of Indians, the United Fund supports small social work and counseling agencies. Minneapolis, with an Indian population of 12,000, has such a center, as have Chicago and Phoenix. Not even the most lenient critic could judge philanthropy to be effective in mitigating our disgraceful treatment of this minority.

Our citizens of Oriental ancestry have received little assistance from "white" philanthropy. Originally, Japanese immigrants were assisted by the *Kenjin-kai*, organizations of people from the same *ken* or prefecture, and by the Christian and Buddhist churches. Following the brutal treatment meted out to Japanese Americans during World War II, the dominant voluntary group assisting these people was the Japanese-American Citizens League. It has about 30,000 members in approximately 100 chapters, mostly on the West Coast but also in such population centers as Washington, New York, Philadelphia, Chicago, and St. Louis. The organization is concerned with the social, political, and cultural welfare of this minority. As

in the case of the Jewish self-help organizations, donations
come largely from members, not from foundations or individuals outside the ethnic group.[5]

In one state, Hawaii, Japanese Americans require little
help. Currently, both the Governor and the Lieutenant
Governor are of Japanese extraction. Both houses of the
state legislature have Japanese majorities. Three of the
state's four federal legislative representatives have Japanese origins, and the fourth (Senator Fong) has Chinese
antecedents.

Chinese Americans represent less than 1 percent of our
population, but because of their concentration in the
Chinatowns of large cities, they are a highly visible minority. As early as the 1900s, the Chinese-American Citizens
Alliance formed to fight discrimination, but today many
feel that its successes over the years have made it com-
placent. A more militant group, Chinese for Affirmative
Action, recently formed in San Francisco (where there are
70,000 Chinese Americans) to concentrate on ending discrimination in employment. It is a relatively small organization with a $20,000 annual budget, but it reports that
progress is being made.[6]

The country's second-largest minority group, Mexican
Americans, is in many ways even more disadvantaged
than the blacks. The Census Bureau admits that its 1970
figure of 5.1 million for this group is inaccurate, as it
omits all illegal immigrants and many women married to
Anglos. The current estimate is closer to 7.5 million.[7]
The vast majority of Chicanos live in cities and therefore
face urban problems. Handicapped by a language barrier,
the average Chicano is poor (the Census Bureau estimated

the median income as less than 70 percent of that of the general population) and is faced with an unemployment rate double the national figure. Chicanos as a group receive only slightly over half the education that Anglos do, and in all states, the average black attends school longer than his Mexican-American counterpart.[8]

Because virtually no economic middle class of this minority exists, Chicano-supported philanthropy is scant. Taking a page from the blacks' aggressive civil-rights movement of the 1960s, Chicanos have organized in a number of cities to improve their lot through politics and application of community pressures. Led by students, the Chicano movement started as a protest, but its own dynamics led it into cultural nationalism. The Ford Foundation has been a leader in supporting Chicano groups in various cities with grants totaling over $5 million through 1971. More recently, in 1973, the Foundation stepped up its support by making grants to Chicano organizations in Phoenix, San Antonio, Oakland, Los Angeles, and to the National Council of La Raza, the coordinating group for the various local organizations. Organizing assistance and some financial support have also come from American Protestant denominations, notably the National Council of Churches.

The plight of this minority does not seem to touch the conscience of white Americans so deeply as that of either the blacks or the Indians. Mexican Americans were living in what is now the southwestern part of the United States before that land was seized or purchased from Mexico. Even those who emigrated here much later did so voluntarily. The emotional appeal that facilitates fund raising is lacking, but thoughtful donors should direct far larger sums of philanthropic money to the self-help projects of the Chicanos as they struggle toward equality.

The problems of the 1.5 million Puerto Ricans on the mainland, most of whom live in New York City, are similar to those besetting the other Spanish-speaking minority.[9] Hampered by the language barrier and suffering further from inadequate educational facilities, the great majority have a minimal earning capacity. The unemployment rate for this ethnic group is double the average for the city as a whole. With virtually no middle class, the Puerto Ricans are unable to mount any meaningful philanthropic effort on their own behalf. What voluntary remedial activities exist are largely conducted by various churches, which direct educational anti-drug campaigns and some social work activities. An increasing number of Puerto Ricans have taken office in New York's municipal government, and they have encouraged a number of local self-help projects.

The economic, educational, and social problems facing all the minority groups are far too massive to be more than slightly mitigated, let alone solved, by philanthropy. Even government, with its vast powers and huge expenditures, seems unable to do much beyond assuring survival at minimum levels of housing, health care, and education. Only the naive believe that all human dilemmas are solvable. Unfortunately, some problems are so huge that they do not disappear; somehow men just learn to live with them. The apathetic acceptance by the overwhelming majority of the plight of these minority groups assures that the present problems will long be with us.

CHAPTER 14

Saving Our Heritage for the Future

MOST PHILANTHROPY IS DIRECTED toward alleviating current problems. Only recently have thousands of thoughtful people, looking into the future, organized to save the environment for our heirs. While America was expanding westward, survival depended on leveling forests, killing wildlife, building roads and railroads, and in every way using nature's bounty for man's gain. There is no need to catalogue again what has happened to our wilderness areas, our streams, our wildlife, and the very air we breathe. No American who has eyes to see can fail to notice how, during our own lifetimes, industrialization has altered the environment, which took nature millions of years to create. A few concerned citizens in the late nineteenth century formed tiny organizations to combat the pillage, but the twentieth century reached its midpoint before larger groups with more powerful voices waged combat with the developers' age-old slogan — "You can't stop progress." By the 1970s, more than 150 national organizations and thousands of local groups existed to promote various facets of conservation and to protest increasing pollution.[1] Students and politicians joined the bird watchers and the hikers in the fight to protect the ecology.

The earliest conservation organizations were formed to preserve the forests from the ravages of the lumber companies. The American Forestry Association was founded in 1875 to advance intelligent management and use of our natural resources, but from its beginnings this group has been more interested in the *use* and the renewable growth of our forests than in their preservation. In 1892, the Sierra Club organized "to explore, enjoy, and preserve the Sierra Nevada and other scenic resources." This effort, limited in scope to the Pacific Coast in its early years, expanded its areas of interest and its membership greatly when general concern developed during the late 1960s. The Save-the-Redwoods League was started in 1918 with the primary purpose of preserving groves of these stately trees in permanent parks. State and federal governments cooperated despite the opposition of lumber interests, and today the League accepts gifts, with which it purchases additional redwood stands to be deeded over to the California Park Commission. The Nature Conservancy, founded at about the same time as the League, adopted similar methods to achieve wider objectives. Rather than limiting itself to one species of tree, "it seeks by gift or purchase, to acquire tracts that are important for scientific, scenic, or educational reasons." By 1968, the Conservancy had acquired 85,000 acres, including forests, prairies, swamps, marshes, seashores, and islands. In 1974, a gift of 25,000 acres of South Carolina ocean front, valued at about $20 million, was added to the Conservancy's growing inventory of sanctuaries and preserves.[2] As an indication of the growing interest in this effort, the South Carolina acquisition brought to 690,000 acres the total lands in forty-seven states under the responsibility of the Conservancy.

Simultaneously with the early twentieth-century effort to save wilderness areas, voluntary groups formed to protect wildlife. The National Audubon Society, by all odds the best known and richest of this group, was founded in 1905. Although its principal concern has been bird life, it recognizes the interdependence of animals and their natural habitats, and conducts general research and public education projects as part of its program. Other organizations began as crusades against cruel methods of trapping; as laws came into force regulating these practices, these groups shifted to protecting endangered species and preserving present sanctuaries.

The area of wildlife protection clearly illustrates how philanthropy, entering a field of social interest, is limited in effectiveness when the problem is so large that government action is necessary to effect a remedy. Conservation societies can, and do, lament the slaughter of predatory animals — the wolf, fox, coyote, hawk, osprey, etc. — and try to educate the public concerning the necessary role that these creatures play in nature's scheme by thinning out the weak from the herds and maintaining the balance of nature. But no amount of education and repeated pleas for mercy will ultimately prove effective; only the passage of ever more stringent game laws, limitations on hunting seasons, and formation of wildlife sanctuaries will finally protect these creatures.

Another facet of the struggle to defend the ecology leaves only a minor role for philanthropy to play. The causes of and even cures for the many forms of pollution are being studied by research groups at many major universities. Schools of public health and medical schools publish their findings and educate the public as well as their students regarding the hazards in present methods of disposing of human and industrial wastes. Some of the more important research projects are funded by philanthropic grants, but only government has sufficient power to order a halt to harmful practices. The non-tax-exempt organizations can lobby to persuade government to act, but apart from research, it is nearly impossible for a tax-exempt group to be effective in the struggle to restore clean air, clean streams, and even to stop polluting oceans.

Philanthropy is still able to make a contribution in one of the most important facets of the conservation movement, population control. Because of strong religious beliefs held by large segments of the population, government is loath to encourage research or to support programs dealing with birth control. Yet many ecologists contend that without major steps in slowing population growth, all efforts to minimize pollution are futile. Dr. Paul Ehrlich at Stanford University voiced this viewpoint: "I do not say all the problems of the world are caused by population, but whatever your cause, it's a lost cause without population control."[3] In 1830, the world population was 1 billion; by 1930 there were 2 billion; by 1960 there were 3 billion; as this is being written there are 3.5 billion; and by the late seventies there will be 4 billion. If this rate of growth continues, the population will be 7 billion by the close of this century. In our own country, by 1917 there were 100 million Americans; by 1967 there were 200 million; and by the year 2000 there will be 300 million. These figures take on a frightening reality when we realize that one baby is born every twelve seconds; one automobile is completed every five seconds; and one acre of land is paved for roads or converted to residential or commercial purposes every thirty seconds. As ex-President Nixon asked in his "Message on Population" on July 18, 1969, "Where will the next hundred million Americans live?" How will they be housed? What of our natural resources and the quality of our environment? How will we educate, employ, transport, and provide health care for all these newcomers, when our present facilities are already inadequate? Nixon did not discover this problem; he merely voiced a concern to which demographers have been trying to alert us for decades.

Despite opposition from important religious groups, particularly the Catholic Church, philanthropic organizations have sponsored research in the medical aspects of birth control. The research that led to the pill and the coil, as well as to public education in their use, was largely sponsored by philanthropy. Planned Parenthood, the largest organization espousing controlled population, led the way, but many other smaller groups helped out. These agencies also lent their support to the fight for liberalized abortion laws, despite its political overtones. It would be absurd to grant the philanthropic groups sole credit for the spectacular decrease in the birth rate over the last few years, but without a doubt they are one factor. While America's population will continue to grow in the next seventy-five years before it levels off, much of the increase will be due to longevity rather than to a runaway birth rate as in the past. However, even if America attains zero growth by 2050, as demographers now predict, the population control groups have endless tasks ahead in trying to bring knowledge and modern techniques to foreign countries, particularly the underdeveloped nations of the world. It will probably be centuries before the ancient scourges of famine, war, and pestilence give way to scientific methods of controlling population growth. As in almost all other philanthropic undertakings, it is virtually impossible to judge accurately how effective the work of the voluntary population agencies is in this enormously complex area, but it is certain that the challenges they are facing will persist in the foreseeable future.

When organizations dedicated to the many aspects of conservation found themselves increasingly calling on legislators for help, and as pleas turned to more persuasive lobbying, their tax-exempt status became threatened. The line between the granting of tax exemption and refusing it is narrow and must give the Commissioner of Internal Revenue considerable pause in particular cases. The Audubon Society supports all measures that protect bird life, openly opposes any pollution of our waters that threatens birds, and recommends measures to preserve species that are in danger of extinction; the Society enjoys exemption. The Sierra Club, with its somewhat broader objectives, in that birds are not the central focus of its conservation efforts, ran afoul of the Internal Revenue Code in late 1966. During the sixties, the Club became more militant in opposing freeways, dams, and lumber company practices; so the Commissioner determined that its political activities rendered it ineligible for continued tax exemption. The Sierra Club promptly activated a subsidiary foundation created in 1960 "to carry out the . . . charitable, scientific, literary, and educational work of the Sierra Club." The Foundation is tax-exempt because it meticulously avoids lobbying. The device of creating a tax-exempt foundation to conduct research, finance legal fees, and strive to educate the public — all to the benefit of a non-tax-exempt lobbying organization — has become a standard device to circumvent the fuzzy boundaries of the Internal Revenue Code.

Conservationists do not stand alone in their willingness to surrender tax exemption in order to achieve reform by supporting legislation. Paradoxically, voluntary organizations that seek to improve governmental machinery are ineligible for the blessing of tax exemption. The nonpartisan League of Women Voters, for example, supports no party and no candidate in elections. However, it seeks through the dissemination of detailed biographical material on office seekers to educate voters. The League was founded in 1920, the year when women's suffrage became part of the Constitution, and many of the same women who had fought for the right to vote organized the new League to inform the recently enfranchised voters regarding the candidates and the issues on the ballot. Today the League (which now admits men to membership) has about 157,000 members in more than 1275 local Leagues in all the states and territories. The League is financed by membership dues, which furnish one fourth of the budget, and contributions, which supply the rest. The League spends about $35 million annually, of which local Leagues spend about one half and the state and national Leagues divide the remainder. The League concentrates on such subjects as the adequacy of schools, environmental protection, housing, and international cooperation to promote peace. "League membership is predominantly composed of middle-class, middle-aged whites. The very rich, the very poor, and the young, for the most part, do not join the League."[4] The League has established a tax-exempt instrument, the League of Women Voters Education Fund, which is devoted solely to research and education.

The American Civil Liberties Union, founded in 1920, has attracted a membership of around 170,000 whose dues and contributions finance the ACLU's work. It has 47 regional or state affiliates and 325 local chapters, which receive about half the money. Its total non-tax-exempt income is around $2.5 million per year, and its tax-exempt counterpart, the ACLU Foundation, receives a similar amount. The ACLU supplies counsel to those who it believes have been denied their civil liberties; this frequently occurs in unpopular cases in which the defendant is advocating revolution or atheism or any of a dozen generally unacceptable goals. It has participated in such widely disparate legal defenses as the conspiracy trials of Dr. Benjamin Spock and Father Daniel Berrigan on one hand and, on the other, the John Birch Society's right to hold parades. It also submits friend-of-the-court briefs in certain cases, even though the defendant has his own lawyer. The ACLU also openly opposes new laws or regulations that it believes infringe on civil liberties, and it engages in popular education for the purpose of building pressure against such laws and regulations. Because the ACLU is forced to select the cases in which it assists, it is frequently involved in controversy both from within and from without.

The wavering boundary line between tax exemption and its denial are best illustrated in the conglomerate of "do good" endeavors headed by crusader Ralph Nader. A lawyer by training, Nader uses the courts to correct abuses affecting consumers but also has become skilled in publicizing affronts to the public interest through the press and in magazine articles and books published under his aegis. Nader's core organization, which employs the senior members of the staff, is the Center for Study of Responsive Law, a tax-exempt body that receives support from both foundations and individuals; as of 1971 its annual budget was $300,000. This organization studies the areas in which consumer affairs are being mishandled and suggests countermeasures to correct failings. The Public Interest Research Group, another Nader offspring, is not tax-exempt and is financed by Nader's lecture fees and his $280,000 out-of-court award from General Motors resulting from his successful libel suit against that company. Spin-offs of this central body include the Center for Auto Safety, which receives two thirds of its budget from the magazine *Consumer's Union*, the Corporate Accountability Research Group, the Aviation Consumer Action Project, the Clearinghouse for Professional Responsibility, and Public Citizen, Inc. Because changes in current laws and the government's administrative procedures are the objectives for reform, these organizations do not enjoy tax exemption. Nader solicits voluntary support through direct mail and newspaper advertisements for both his tax-exempt and non-tax-exempt groups. His record of accomplishment is impressive. His personal dedication and the skill and energy of his staff have made many friends for his various endeavors as well as an impressive list of enemies.

The closeness of Internal Revenue's decisions on tax exemption was demonstrated in 1970 by a sudden about-face. In that year, the IRS suspended the tax exemption of so-called "public interest" organizations of lawyers, such as the one headed by Ralph Nader. These groups bring actions in the name of the public toward such objectives as protecting consumers, preventing and controlling pollution, requiring that broadcasting engage in public service, and eliminating discrimination. The revocation of tax exemption was prompted by the notion that legal service to the poor — such as that sponsored by the Legal Aid Society — was distinguishable from court action against corporations polluting the environment, the first being charitable and the second not. IRS officials questioned whether it was "fair" for lawyers supported by tax-deductible contributions to oppose lawyers paid by corporate funds. It soon became apparent that choices could not be made on this basis; within five weeks the tax exemption was restored, with the result that organizations for public interest legal action are now accepted as tax-exempt so long as they are not a cloak for lobbying or for service to private interests. Many diverse factions rallied to the defense of the public interest organizations. Congressmen of both parties, the press, foundations, and the public interest lawyers themselves mounted an articulate protest at the suspension and made it short-lived.

Voluntary groups that lobby openly in the public interest and use all of the techniques of mass education, rather than the courts, to effect reform do not seek tax exemption. One of them, Common Cause, founded in 1968, is essentially the offspring of one man, John Gardner, who was Secretary of Health, Education and Welfare in the Johnson administration and before that the President of the Carnegie Corporation. The overall if somewhat fuzzy purpose of Common Cause is general governmental reform in order to restore legislative responsiveness to the public's desires. Many think that the organization is either merely the base for the founding of a third political party or a platform for Gardner's own political ambitions in one of the established parties. Gardner denies both intentions. With membership dues at $15 a year, Common Cause attracted over 100,000 members within a year of its establishment, and by 1973, 215,000 dues payers had joined.

Organizations striving for peace constitute a mixed bag of tax-exempt and non-tax-exempt bodies. If a group is for peace in general, like the Carnegie Endowment for International Peace, it is tax-exempt. If it is for a particular peace — ending the war in Vietnam, for example — it probably does not enjoy tax exemption, because to be effective it would have to lobby for congressional action to deny appropriations or for a congressional resolution to end the war by a certain date. Thus SANE, which was founded after World War II to encourage nuclear disarmament but later became active in lobbying against the Vietnam war, is not tax-exempt. However, the Fund for

Peace, established in 1967 while the Vietnam war was raging, limits itself to education and research and thus is tax-exempt.

Only churches are secure in retaining their tax-exempt status regardless of their lobbying activities. The opposition of the Catholic Church to laws liberalizing abortion or promoting the availability of contraceptive devices is consistent and powerful. Organized Jewry supports federal aid to Israel whenever appropriations are discussed. Various Protestant sects make no secret of their opposition when legislation is being considered to render financial aid to parochial schools.

When considering gifts to groups that use political pressure to preserve our environment, to clean up our politics, to reform our governmental structure, or to protect consumers from shady practices, donors to the non-tax-exempt groups can be said to be the purest philanthropists. They receive only the satisfaction of assisting in a worthy cause without even the benefit of tax forgiveness to make giving less painful. Furthermore, I believe it can be successfully argued that whether a voluntary group's purpose is to preserve the wilderness or to protect our ancient liberties, the most effective method is through pressure on government. The defense of our land and our heritage has always called for sacrifice. In war the sacrifice may involve our lives; during peace it involves only money.

Unmet Needs and Guides to Giving

MANY AMERICANS STILL CHERISH the concept, fostered by our history, that concerned citizens voluntarily working together can respond satisfactorily to all our social needs. De Tocqueville commented on this national trait in the early nineteenth century:

> In no country in the world has the principle of association been more successfully used, or applied to a greater multitude of objects, than in America. Besides the permanent associations, which are established by law . . . a vast number of others are formed and maintained by the agency of private individuals. The citizen of the United States is taught from infancy to rely upon his own exertions.[1]

In that predominantly rural society with its ever-expanding frontier, community action was the only possible response to the demands for education, assistance for the old and needy, and care for the sick. In today's highly industrialized urban structure, there survives only the heritage and the memory of voluntary action as a remedy to social ills. No longer is it true that America's most urgent needs remain voluntary philanthropy's top priority. Whether we observe the plight of the poor in our metropolitan ghettos or bewail the fact that several million Americans are illiterate, we are forced to conclude that our major problems are too large for voluntary philanthropy to do much more than study. Donors want to give where the need is greatest, but their offerings have a negligible impact in correcting the greatest flaws of today's complex society. What we require in the last quarter of the twentieth century is not the abolition of philanthropy because it is no longer effective in its traditional role, but a reassessment of what voluntary action can still accomplish in a modern setting.

If we lived in Utopia, we could immediately redirect the flow of philanthropy's money to achieve maximum benefits in minimum time. Effective reform is rarely accomplished by beginning all over again, and even if it were, good reasons exist why such a revolutionary approach would be undesirable. Both the donor and the recipient are necessary to create philanthropy, and the donor's priority cannot be disregarded entirely in order to magnify the recipient's share. The donor's act in giving money or time as a volunteer has social value. In an era of big and impersonal government, many individuals have discovered that personal involvement in community affairs can be achieved only through philanthropic activity. Quite apart from the benefits flowing outward from the gifts of time or money, the donor learns in detail the needs of his agency's beneficiaries and in a general way the broader social needs of the entire community. To sacrifice this educational process in the interest of total efficiency would be wasteful.

Currently, perhaps 98 percent of all philanthropic donations go to already established institutions in order to maintain ongoing programs. Once a donor has been persuaded to give to the local United Fund or the American Cancer Society, he is likely to respond to subsequent annual appeals by repeating or enlarging his gift. Many of these programs undoubtedly merit continued support, but, as we have seen, a substantial number have outlived their usefulness because of massive government intervention or because their original goal has been achieved. The opportunity to redirect the flow of philanthropic dollars to achieve greater benefits lies in the donor's initiative.

If the individual donor is willing to make the general policy decision of re-examining his annual contributions, he is confronted with problems of choice as to where to cut down and where to increase his donations. He may feel that his information is inadequate for him to make intelligent decisions and may be unaware that agencies exist to provide pertinent information. Obviously, no one wants to contribute to an out-and-out charity racket — of which relatively few exist. The general statutes regarding fraud protect the donor, and, in addition, twenty-five states and the District of Columbia have laws of varying toughness regarding the solicitation of charitable funds. Many municipalities also have laws on their books, though the funds for effective enforcement are generally skimpy.

Apart from abhorring real rackets, of which the Sister Elizabeth Kenny Foundation with its $16 million fraud in the 1950s furnishes an historic example,[2] people do not want to give to organizations which spend an excessive proportion of their incomes raising additional funds. Unfortunately, there are many of these, and the question arises as to how much is too much to spend to raise more. The city of Los Angeles has a rule that no more than 20 percent of an agency's annual income can be spent on fund raising. The state of Pennsylvania, in what has been described as the "toughest" state law regulating charity yet passed, allows 35 percent of income to be spent attracting funds. Few would agree with ex-President Nixon's commendation in 1970 of the Disabled American Veterans if they knew that 63 percent of this organization's income was spent raising money. In 1972, the Epilepsy Foundation of America spent nearly half of its $2.5 million income to raise funds. The American Lung Association (Christmas Seal) spent 44 percent of its take on management and fund raising.

One of the simplest rules to follow for those who do not wish to see a major share of their contributions go to raising further funds is never to respond to appeals containing merchandise, stamps, coins, or any other enclosure of value. Fund-raising campaigns which utilize the technique of enclosing some article in mail solicitation are notoriously high-cost operations. As a matter of fact, a good many fly-by-night agencies would be eliminated and the U.S. mail less burdened if everybody declined to respond to mass mailing solicitation. An agency of any kind can purchase lists of names with addresses and send out thousands of appeals in the hope of attracting sufficient response to pay at least for the mailing. To say that this is a wasteful method is understatement. The response of the donor to direct mail solicitation is either to discard the appeal in the wastebasket or at best to make a small $5 or $10 contribution. The fact is that contributions of less than $25, unless they are dues in an organization or museum to which the donor belongs, hardly advance the activities of the soliciting agency. By the time lists are purchased, addressing machine plates are cut or, if borrowed, run off, postage is paid, and the labor involved is compensated, direct mail costs perhaps $3 or more per letter. Thus small contributions merely compensate the solicitor for creating the nuisance of mass mailing.

Warnings of where *not* to give will not assist those who wish to contribute to worthy causes, but positive methods do exist which make evaluation relatively easy. All worthwhile agencies draw up audited annual financial reports and will make them available upon request. These reports disclose what proportions of funds go to administration, to fund raising, to public education, to research, and to the clients. While many agencies tend to obscure their administrative costs by splitting them into a number of headings, any careful reader can ascertain the truth. If an agency declines to furnish its information on request, it does not deserve a contribution. In the twenty states which have registration laws for solicitation, these reports are on file and available to the public from the governmental bureau established to receive them. An inquiry to the Secretary of State or to a constituent's legislative representative will disclose what information is available and how to obtain it.

For donors who wish to investigate a number of established causes before making their choice, the National Information Bureau, 419 Park Avenue South, New York, N.Y. 10016, provides a convenient central source of information. For a small annual fee, which itself is tax-deductible, an individual can become a member of this organization. He is then privileged to request reports on any of the more than 500 organizations which solicit funds for national or international programs. The reports by this objective agency include statements of income and expenditure as well as comments on frequency of trustees meetings, programs, and other pertinent information. The small membership fee in this organization is an excellent investment for all who wish to avoid unwise gifts to unworthy causes.

Techniques for avoiding gifts to unworthy causes constitute only a minor aspect of intelligent giving. Far more important is the selection of the general areas of endeavor in which donations will have the most beneficial effect. Nearly all fund-raising appeals are strident and imply that disaster will strike if additional funds are not made available. It is therefore incumbent on donors to establish their own priority order before selecting particular agencies. People of middle age or older — the majority of those with money to give — find it difficult to accept the fact that the causes that had the greatest urgency in past years are no longer in need. The refusal to renew an oft-repeated annual donation is an unpleasant decision to make, similar to terminating a long-time friendship. Nevertheless, philanthropic priorities, like past loyalties, should be periodically reassessed. In the hope of stimulating thought on this most important aspect of tomorrow's philanthropy, I include in the following survey my own conclusions, formed after several years of research, regarding the directions in which future philanthropy could more intelligently flow.

United Way — Local United Way campaigns raise nearly $1 billion annually and distribute funds to such well-established organizations as the Red Cross, the Boy Scouts, local social work agencies, and the major health agencies. Nearly 62 percent of the money raised comes from payroll deductions pledged through annual in-plant solicitation. Corporations give 29 percent to United Funds in localities where they do business. Individuals and foundations contribute a little over 9 percent of the total. There can be no valid argument against sustaining agencies that have proven their value over the years, but it is clear that the employee solicitation conducted on company premises plus gifts from corporations dictated by public relations considerations should assure the continuity of United Fund participants. It would seem that individuals who wish to shift priorities to more innovative programs might be well advised to review the amounts they presently give to their United Fund appeals.

Health Agencies — Philanthropic donations to voluntary health care agencies come to only 1½ percent of the national total expended. In 1973, Americans spent over $83 billion for medical and hospital services, drugs, appliances, and equipment, of which $48 billion was paid for by individuals or through Blue Cross and other insurance plans. Of the remaining $35 billion, the thirty-four largest health agencies contributed 1.1 percent, all other foundations and non-profit groups 5.9 percent, and federal, state, and local governments 93 percent. Considering the relatively high costs (approximately 30 cents of each dollar) of raising gifts, and the small proportion of expenditures that result, I would award donations to the health agencies the lowest priority. The splintering in this field, the lack of overall planning, the inter-agency competition for the donor's dollar — all tend to reduce the effectiveness of gifts. No other aspect of philanthropy so richly rewards the hard-sell techniques of fund raising with such limited resulting benefits.

Hospitals — The financial problems of our major voluntary hospitals are far beyond the ability of philanthropy to solve. Contributions to annual deficits are insignificant. Of the $32.5 billion Americans expended on hospital care in a recent year, 53 percent came from government, 36 percent came from Blue Cross or commercial insurance plans, 8 percent from direct payments by patients, and only a little over 1 percent came from voluntary organizations, including the hospitals themselves. The simple truth is that our society is not going to permit these lifesaving institutions to close, no matter how difficult their financial problems become. Major philanthropic contributions as equity capital for needed new construction or replacement of outmoded buildings are still useful. Smaller gifts, but still large in size, are required by some hospitals in order to establish innovative research programs, which, if they prove to be promising, will receive continued support from government grants. With some type of national health insurance a legislative certainty in the near future, the time is past for philanthropy to play more than a tiny part in hospital financing.

Religion — Nearly half of today's total contributions goes to religious causes. To urge any reassessment of religious gifts would be foolhardy as well as futile. People's loyalty to the church that offers them spiritual guidance and to the religious faith that prompts their generosity is far too important an ingredient of human happiness to be a subject for intellectual analysis. America's churches are in trouble. Declining attendance, a general falling-off of religious interest, and the undermining of traditional ethical standards for human behavior have all had their effect, along with inflation, on church finances. Certainly the donor who contributes his tithe to the church of his choice does not have to investigate the integrity of the recipient. Members of a sect have the privilege and the duty of debating the usefulness of their church's social programs; for an outsider to indulge in the exercise is gratuitous. Where constitutional or legal questions become involved, as in the debate over government support for parochial schools or freedom of access to abortion, all citizens may properly take sides through use of the ballot. Apart from a few broad issues of this kind, advice on the wisdom of religious philanthropic programming is probably unneeded and certainly unwanted.

Child Care and Recreation — The mails are flooded with appeals on behalf of children. They may be depicted as starving in Korea, deserted in New Mexico, or suffering a crippling illness almost anywhere. Compassion must trigger responses, or the thousands upon thousands of dollars spent on these mailings would cease. The most reputable of the voluntary agencies do not stoop to these tear-jerking tactics but receive most of their philanthropic gifts through sectarian federated fund drives or the United Way. Philanthropy's role in alleviating child care problems is constantly diminishing, because government funds are available to maintain necessary programs. Today, public financing is so dominant that most of the classic arguments favoring pluralism are irrelevant, except in regard to those agencies devoted to monitoring the multiplicity of programs and offering constructive criticism to achieve better results.

The recreation field for children and youth presents a different picture. Programs conducted for the offspring of the middle class by scouting, the Y's, and other similar organizations do require gifts, but it would seem that parents of those involved should meet these needs as fees for services rendered. Quite apart from any payments from parents, the United Way allocates around $200 million a year to recreational programs. I can see every reason why the families of children who benefit by these activities should contribute, and very little reason for anyone else to do so.

The Arts and Humanities — Gifts to cultural causes do not offer the donor the ego satisfaction that accompanies similar sums to child care institutions, but on a logical basis they deserve a higher priority. Government support, although growing in size, is only a small segment of what is required. Other industrial nations, although not as affluent as the United States, devote a far larger share of tax monies to support the arts. The relatively inexpensive membership dues solicited by local museums are tax-deductible, and permit attendance at exhibits without additional charge. Educational television stations also deserve the support of viewers who enjoy the programs. I believe that such annual membership dues are one of the best small philanthropic investments. But as opposed to collections such as libraries and museums, the financial problems facing the performing arts are so massive that small donations to a favorite opera company, dance group, or symphony have little impact. However, to the large donor, the foundation, or the corporation, support to this type of endeavor should be attractive. People will not die if the arts starve, but cultural undernourishment is a civilized society's equivalent of individual malnutrition.

Education — No seminar on philanthropic activity would be complete without a number of speakers praising our "pluralistic" society wherein government and voluntary action offer alternative programs. It seems to me that in many fields this hoary platitude has lost its validity. It is clear, however, that private education sets the standards which public education strives to emulate. There are only a few state universities (the University of California at Berkeley is one) that rival the Ivy League universities in academic excellence. It is imperative that the private universities maintain their standard-setting pace, and to achieve this goal philanthropic support is required. At the other end of the scale lie the hard-pressed Negro colleges. In my opinion, the highest philanthropic priority should be given to the United Negro College Fund. In the same connection, donations to the many scholarship funds that allow children of poor parents to attend private colleges are a most useful form of support. Private education from the kindergarten level up to the postgraduate professional school needs every bit of philanthropic encouragement it can attract from alumni and outsiders. Here is one field where those who praise pluralism are exactly correct.

Racial Minorities — Some problems are not only too great for philanthropy to solve, they are insolvable given the nature of the human animal. Discrimination by reason of race, creed, and color has been present for centuries, and the headlines each morning are a daily reminder of the continuing defeats of the ideals we supposedly endorse. This is not to say that nothing should be done. The NAACP, its tax-exempt foundation for research, and the Urban League should receive far greater funds from people of good will than they do. Equally important are those agencies which seek to improve the Spanish-speaking population's educational opportunities, for only thus will future generations be able to establish the self-help facilities that can guarantee a more equal fight against injustice and discrimination.

Conservation — Gifts to most causes answer an immediate need and are quickly spent to meet it. Gifts to the major conservation agencies are an investment in the future and their benefits are cumulative. Nature Conservancy, Save-the-Redwoods League, the Audubon Society, and various historical associations dedicated to preserving famous sites perform an invaluable service for our heirs by acquiring land. The more wilderness areas rescued from the real estate developers' ministrations and exploitation by commercial ravagers, the greater will be the value of life for our successors. Philanthropy can serve only as a minor palliative to our social ills or as a temporary cure for urgent needs. Government must intervene if meaningful progress is to be made, and this is particularly true in the area of conservation. Organizations such as the Sierra Club, which surrendered its tax exemption in order to be free to spur government to action, deserve the support of concerned ecologists. Local groups formed to protect a swamp, a forest, or a prairie are also effective instruments for guarding our heritage. In the last analysis, government, and government alone, has the power to stop the pollution of our atmosphere, our streams, and our oceans. Legislatures move when they are prodded and the non-tax-exempt philanthropic agencies are free to prod. Dollars given to such groups as those headed by Ralph Nader and to associations like the League of Women Voters, the American Civil Liberties Union, and countless others that strive to make government responsive to public needs are in many ways the most valuable and the most needed of gifts.

American philanthropy, for all of its vast size, is not large enough to maintain urgent programs. Part of the problem is that donors decline to distinguish between traditional demands and current needs. When we consider how much time and energy is spent in the accumulation of wealth, it would seem high time that more thought be given to its distribution. An investor, seeking profits, could hardly be expected to purchase stock in a company formed to restore clipper ships to international trading. Yet some philanthropic organizations, still successful at raising funds, are as out of step with modern needs as the stately ships that used wind alone for propulsion. If donors examined causes with the same care as investors do, the flow of philanthropic dollars would have far more impact. As this is being written, our country appears to be entering another period of serious economic decline. With job security uncertain, with salaries and income from other sources reduced, with inflation accompanying recession, donors will unquestionably be forced to reduce the size of their contributions and to reassess the usefulness of their gifts. Such a reassessment is long overdue, and one must hope that the voluntary sector of our society will emerge with more relevance to current needs. Apart from the ballot box, philanthropy presents the one opportunity the individual has to express his meaningful choice over the direction in which our society will progress.

Appendices
Notes
Selected Bibliography
Index

Appendix A

Some Leading U.S. Private Foundations
Ranked by Payment of Grants (000)
Source: *Giving USA*, 1974

Foundation	1973 Grant Payments	Assets at Year-End (Market Value)
Ford F.	$195,753	$ 3,145,579
Rockefeller F.	40,272	838,980
Lilly Endowment, Inc.	31,113	1,138,500
Kresge F.	26,848	657,953
Andrew W. Mellon F.	26,542	647,924
W. K. Kellogg F.	20,092	577,328
Duke Endowment	19,171	366,888
Charles Stewart Mott F.	16,801	323,000
Alfred P. Sloan F.	14,135	284,328
Carnegie Corp. of New York	13,982	338,470
Danforth F.	12,288	197,513
Edna McConnell Clark F.	9,046	262,445
Frank E. Gannett Newspaper F.	7,500	178,000
Commonwealth Fund	7,353	144,940
Moody F.	7,206	113,000
John A. Hartford F., Inc.	6,960	119,005
Houston Endowment, Inc.	6,929	250,000
Haas Community Fund	6,146	162,608
Bush F.	5,883	147,177
Robert A. Welch F.	5,725	108,497
Amon G. Carter F.	4,755	70,000
William R. Kenan, Jr., Charitable Trust	4,662	107,320
Louis W. & Maud Hill Family F.	4,440	118,560
Max C. Fleischmann F.	4,332	103,005
Research Corporation	4,181	91,288
John Simon Guggenheim Memorial F.	4,077	100,510
Charles F. Kettering F.	3,532	92,715
Charles Hayden F.	3,180	79,227
El Pomar F.	3,117	73,700
James Irvine F.	2,874	99,211
Booth Ferris F.	2,820	63,756

Sarah Scaife F., Inc.	2,541	84,640
George Gund F.	2,433	65,512
John & Mary R. Markle F.	2,288	60,053
W. Clement & Jessie V. Stone F.	1,976	1,046
Callaway F., Inc.	1,693	71,107
Henry Luce F., Inc.	1,284	29,663
Elliott White Springs F., Inc.	1,235	18,829
Totals	$535,165	$11,332,277

Note: This listing omits some large corporation foundations as well as the Robert Wood Johnson Foundation, the Richard King Mellon Foundation, the Woodruff Foundation, the Pew Memorial Trust, and the Rockefeller Brothers Fund.

Appendix B1

Major Health Agency Income and Expenditures

Name of Agency	Support Revenue 1973	Expenditures 1973
American Cancer Society	$ 98,387,000-E	$ 83,266,000-E
American Heart Association	60,821,000-E	54,452,000-E
Easter Seal Society	55,000,000-E	52,000,000-E
American Lung Association	44,000,000-E	44,000,000-E
National Foundation	43,557,000	33,957,000
Planned Parenthood	42,000,000-E	42,000,000-E
United Cerebral Palsy Association	27,500,000-E	27,000,000-E
Muscular Dystrophy Associations of America	20,571,000-E	18,436,000-E
National Association for Mental Health	15,600,000-E	15,600,000-E
National Multiple Sclerosis Society	12,121,000-E	10,168,000-E
Arthritis Foundation	10,486,000-E	10,486,000-E
National Association for Retarded Citizens	7,892,000-E	7,985,000-E

Leukemia Society of America	6,427,000	6,169,000
National Cystic Fibrosis Research Foundation	5,961,000	5,541,000
American Foundation for Blind	5,506,000	5,320,000
Epilepsy Foundation of America	5,320,000-E	5,280,000-E
National Kidney Foundation	4,700,000-E	4,000,000-E
National League for Nursing	4,191,000	4,134,000
National Hemophilia Foundation	4,154,000-E	3,905,000-E
Seeing Eye, Inc.	3,298,000	2,097,000
National Council on Alcoholism	3,250,000-E	2,575,000-E
American Diabetes Association	3,135,000-E	3,367,000-E
National Medical Fellowships	2,810,000	2,740,000
National Society for Prevention Blindness	2,750,000-E	2,700,000-E
Recording for the Blind	1,819,000	1,603,000
Damon Runyon–W. Winchell Cancer Fund	1,573,000	2,852,000
American Fund for Dental Health	975,000-E	940,000
National Fund for Medical Education	820,000-E	800,000-E
American Social Health Association	732,000	732,000
Deafness Research Foundation	722,000	425,000
National Association Practical Nurse Education & Service	612,000	639,000
Cancer Research Institute	586,000	691,000
Maternity Center Association	370,000-E	410,000-E
National Association Hearing & Speech Agencies	321,000-E	371,000-E
Allergy Foundation of America	188,000-E	197,000-E
Myasthenia Gravis	156,000-E	208,000-E
Total of 36 national health agencies above	$493,911,000	$457,046,000

E—Estimated by agencies

Appendix B2

Mortality Rate by Diseases
Source: U.S. Public Health Service

Causes of Death	*1972 Death Rate per 100,000*
Cardiovascular diseases (including heart)	493.9
Cancer (malignant neoplasms)	166.6
Accidents	54.6
Influenza and pneumonia	29.4
Diabetes mellitus	18.8
Symptoms and ill-defined conditions (including senility)	17.4
Mortality in early infancy	16.4
Cirrhosis of liver	15.7
Suicide	11.7
Emphysema	10.2
Homicide	9.1
Congenital anomalies (malformations)	7.2
Nephritis and nephrosis	3.9
Peptic ulcer	3.7
Infections of kidney	3.4
Hernia and intestinal obstruction	3.0
Chronic bronchitis	2.6
Tuberculosis	2.2

Appendix B3

Congressional Appropriations for Fiscal 1974

Bureau of Health Resources services administration*	$ 726,845,000**
Mental health*	793,049,000
Cancer	555,191,500
Heart and lung	302,915,000
Arthritis and metabolic diseases	159,447,000
Neurological diseases and stroke	125,000,000
Allergy and infectious diseases	114,000,000
Child health and human development	130,254,000
Dental research	45,565,500
Eye	41,631,000
Environmental health sciences	28,879,000
National Library of Medicine	25,871,000
General medical sciences	176,778,000
Research resources	133,472,000
Miscellaneous	4,767,000
	$3,363,665,000

* Not part of the National Institutes of Health.
** Includes Health Manpower ($688,518,000) and Comprehensive Health Planning ($38,327,000) programs; excludes Hill-Burton Hospital construction.

Notes

INTRODUCTION

1. Table compiled from *Giving, USA 1974, Annual Report*, (New York: American Association of Fund-Raising Counsel, Inc., 1975).
2. Robert Hamlin, *Voluntary Health and Welfare Agencies in the United States* (New York: The Schoolmasters' Press, 1961), p. 2.

CHAPTER 1. *Giving — The Golden Crowbar*

1. David Owen, *English Philanthropy 1660 to 1960* (Cambridge, Mass.: Harvard University Press, Belknap Press, 1964), p. 77.
2. Benedict Nightingale, *Charities* (London: Allen Lane, 1973), p. 100.
3. Dr. Ernest Dichter, "Why People Give" (Paper delivered at 1956 National Biennial Conference of United Community Funds and Councils in Detroit, February 10, 1956).
4. Kenneth E. Boulding, "Notes on a Theory of Philanthropy," ed. Frank G. Dickenson in *Philanthropy and Public Policy* (Washington, D.C.: National Bureau of Economic Research, 1962), p. 57.
5. Jacques Barzun, *The House of Intellect* (New York: Harper Bros., 1959), p. 180.
6. For a detailed discussion with specific examples of this aspect

of the Internal Revenue Code, see Philip M. Stern, *The Great Treasury Raid* (New York: Random House, 1964), chapter 13, " 'Tis More Blessed to Give — If You Work It Right."

7. Merrimon Cuninggim, *Private Money and Public Service — The Role of Foundations in American Society* (New York: McGraw-Hill, 1972), p. 16.
8. *Giving, USA 1973*, p. 12.
9. Quoted in Nightingale, *Charities*, p. 124.

CHAPTER 2. *The Uneasy Marriage — Philanthropy and Government*

1. For an interesting discussion of this development, see *The Quasi Nongovernmental Organization*, a report by Alan Pifer, President of Carnegie Corporation of New York (New York: Carnegie Corporation, 1967).

CHAPTER 3. *Fund Raisers Call the Tune*

1. Arnaud C. Marts, *Philanthropy's Role in Civilization — Its Contribution to Human Freedom* (New York: Harper & Bros., 1953), and *Generosity of Americans: Its Source and Its Achievements* (New York: Prentice-Hall, 1965).
2. Warren Gould, Director of American Alumni Council, quoted in *Business Week*, April 10, 1971.
3. Gustave L. Levy, quoted by Marylin Bender, in "Hard Sell Pays Off in Charity Appeals," *New York Times*, May 5, 1974.

CHAPTER 4. *The United Way — Giving Without Feeling*

1. Scott M. Cutlip, *Fund Raising in the United States* (New Brunswick, N.J.: Rutgers University Press, 1965), pp. 13–18. This book has an excellent history of the early development of federated fund raising.
2. United Way of America, New York, N.Y.
3. John E. Cooney, "Givers, Recipients Assail the United Funds," *Wall Street Journal*, November 25, 1970.
4. Whitney Young, syndicated column, December 3, 1970.
5. *Newsweek*, December 22, 1969.

6. Ibid.
7. William J. Baumol and William G. Bowen, *Performing Arts —
   The Economic Dilemma* (New York: The Twentieth Century
   Fund, 1966), p. 326.
8. *Projections for the Seventies* (New York: United Community
   Funds and Councils of America, 1969), p. 19.

CHAPTER 5. *Trustees — The Abdication of Responsibility*

1. Herman Miles Somers and Anne Ramsay Somers, *Medicare
   and the Hospitals: Issues and Prospects* (Washington, D.C.: The
   Brookings Institution, 1967), p. 52.
2. Morton A. Rauh, "Putting the Trust in Trustees," *Antioch
   Notes*, May 1969.
3. John Kenneth Galbraith, "The Case for Constitutional Reform
   at Harvard," *Harvard Alumni Bulletin*, December 23, 1968.
4. James M. Underwood, "How to Serve on a Hospital Board,"
   Harvard Business Review, July–August 1969.
5. *Report of the Yale University Study Commission* (New Haven:
   Yale University, 1971).
6. Beatrice Dinerman, *The Dynamics of Priority Planning*, A Ford
   Foundation Study (Los Angeles: Welfare Planning Council,
   1965), p. 82.
7. Rodney T. Hartnett, *College and University Trustees* (Prince-
   ton, N.J.: Educational Testing Service, 1969).
8. Rauh, "Putting the Trust in Trustees."

CHAPTER 6. *The Overstressed Foundations*

1. *Giving, USA 1974*, pp. 13, 15.
2. Joseph C. Goulden, *The Money Givers* (New York: Random
   House, 1971).
3. *The Ford Foundation Annual Report, 1967* (New York: Ford
   Foundation, 1968), p. 27.
4. For much fuller discussions of this acrimonious controversy, see
   David Halberstam, "The Very Expensive Education of Mc-
   George Bundy," *Harper's Magazine*, July 1969; and Goulden,
   The Money Givers, chapter 8.
5. *Giving, USA 1974*, p. 17.

6. *National Program Funding and Program Distribution for the Years 1973–74* (New York: Public Broadcasting Service, 1974).
7. *New York Times*, March 26, 1974.
8. *Giving, U.S.A. 1974*, p. 17.
9. *New York Times*, October 13, 1974.
10. Waldemar A. Nielsen, *The Big Foundations* (New York: Columbia University Press, 1972).

CHAPTER 7. *Giving For God's Sake*

1. Scott M. Cutlip, *Fund Raising in the United States*, (New Brunswick, N.J.: Rutgers University Press, 1965), p. viii.
2. Constant H. Jacquet, Jr., ed., *Yearbook of American and Canadian Churches 1973* (New York: Abingdon Press, 1973), pp. 241 f.
3. *Newsweek*, September 9, 1974.
4. Martin A. Larson and C. Stanley Lowell, *Praise the Lord for Tax Exemption* (Washington, D.C.: Robert B. Luce, 1969).
5. Martin A. Larson, *Church Wealth and Business Income* (New York: Philosophical Library, 1965).
6. James Gollin, *Worldly Goods* (New York: Random House, 1971), p. 281.
7. Jacquet, ed., *Yearbook of American and Canadian Churches*, p. 244.
8. Morris Fine and Milton Himmelfarb, eds., *American Jewish Year Book 1972* (New York: The American Jewish Committee, 1972), p. 194 f.
9. *U.S. Dept. of Commerce Construction Review*, March 1973.
10. Gollin, *Worldly Goods*, p. 56.
11. Diane Gertler and Linda Barker, *Statistics of Public and Non Public Elementary and Secondary Day Schools* (Washington, D.C.: Department of Health, Education and Welfare, 1970).
12. *U.S. Catholic Schools 1972–1973* (Washington, D.C.: National Catholic Educational Association, 1973).
13. For a concise history and recent analysis of the parochial school crisis, see Gollin, *Worldly Goods*, pp. 379–418.
14. *Education Directory 1971–72* (Washington, D.C.: U.S. Dept. of Health, Education and Welfare, 1973), Part 3, "Higher Education."

15. *The Independent Catholic College* (Washington, D.C.: National Catholic Educational Association, 1972).
16. Felician A. Foy, OFM, ed., *1974 Catholic Almanac*, (Huntington, Ind.: Our Sunday Visitor, 1973), pp. 610–14.
17. John Cogley, *Catholic America* (New York: Dial Press, 1973), p. 198.
18. Jacquet, ed., *Yearbook of American and Canadian Churches*, p. 263.
19. Fine and Himmelfarb, eds., *American Jewish Year Book 1972*, p. 243.

CHAPTER 8. *Children Are Good Fund Raisers*

1. According to a General Accounting Office report to a Senate subcommittee on children and youth, the Foster Parents Plan of Warwick, Rhode Island, used this misrepresentation. Reported in *Associated Press*, Washington, October 11, 1974.
2. Save the Children Federation, Norwalk, Conn.; ibid.
3. Christian Children's Fund, Richmond, Va.; ibid.
4. Richard Haitch, *Orphans of the Living*, Public Affairs Pamphlet No. 418 (New York: 1968), p. 1.
5. Alfred Kadushin, *Child Welfare Services* (New York: Macmillan, 1967), p. 51.
6. National Center for Social Statistics, *Social and Rehabilitation Service* (Washington, D.C.: U.S. Department of Health, Education and Welfare, 1972).
7. These five statistics from Harry L. Lurie, ed., *Encyclopedia of Social Work* (New York: National Association of Social Workers, 1965), p. 140.
8. Senator Walter F. Mondale, "Think of These Children," *New Republic*, December 26, 1970.
9. David Fanshel and Eugene Shinn, *Dollars and Sense in the Foster Care of Children* (New York: Child Welfare League of America, 1972), pp. 20–21.
10. Carl and Helen Doss-Henny, *If You Adopt a Child* (New York: Henry Holt & Co., 1957), Appendix I.
11. Barbara L. Haring, *Voluntary Member Agency Income 1972–1973* (New York: Child Welfare League of America, 1973), pp. 4 f.

12. For a detailed history of the growth of the YMCA, see C. Howard Hopkins, *History of YMCA in America* (New York: Association Press, 1951).
13. Arthur Hillman, *Neighborhood Centers Today* (New York: National Federation of Settlements and Neighborhood Centers, 1960).

CHAPTER 9. *The Overneedy Hospitals*

1. *Annual Report, 1973* (Chicago, Ill.: American Hospital Association, 1974).
2. *Business Week*, October 26, 1974.
3. Ibid.
4. American Hospital Association, *Annual Report, 1973*.

CHAPTER 10. *The Health Agencies Live on Death*

1. Selskar M. Gunn and Philip S. Platt, *Voluntary Health Agencies* (New York: Ronald Press, 1945), p. 15.
2. Robert H. Hamlin, *Voluntary Health and Welfare Agencies in the United States* (New York: The Schoolmasters' Press, 1961), p. i.
3. Ibid., pp. 35 f.
4. National Health Council, New York, N.Y. The National Health Council was founded in 1920 by a group of leaders who anticipated a vast expansion in health activities and foresaw the chaos that would develop unless health agencies had a mechanism for working together. From an initial membership of ten agencies, the Council has expanded to a membership of over sixty national organizations, including voluntary and governmental health agencies, professional and other membership associations, as well as civic organizations and business groups that have strong health interests.

CHAPTER 11. *The Starving Arts*

1. Up to December 1, 1970, the Main Reading Rooms were open Monday–Saturday, 9 A.M.–10 P.M.; Sundays and holidays,

1 P.M.–10 P.M. They are now open Monday–Saturday, 9 A.M.–
9 P.M.; closed Sundays and holidays.

2. *New York Times,* September 26, 1969.

3. Dillon Ripley, *The Sacred Grove — Essays on Museums* (New
York: Simon & Schuster, 1969), p. 156.

4. National Endowment for the Arts, *Museums USA: Highlights*
(Washington, D.C.: U.S. Government Printing Office, 1973).

5. *New York Times,* January 6, 1971.

6. Interview with Eric Larrabee, Executive Director, N.Y. State
Council on Arts, *New York Times,* February 25, 1974.

7. The facts in this section were taken from a report of the pro-
ceedings of the Conference of Presidents of Symphony Orchestras by Amyas Ames, Chairman of the Committee-on-the-
Whole, in "The Silent Spring of Our Symphonies," *Saturday
Review,* September 28, 1970.

8. John H. Mueller, *The American Symphony Orchestra* (Bloom-
ington, Ind.: Indiana University Press, 1951), p. 78.

9. For a detailed discussion of this situation, see Robert Finklea,
"What Sank the Dallas Symphony Orchestra," *New York
Times,* June 9, 1974.

10. *Business Week,* October 13, 1973.

11. *New York Times,* February 6, 1974.

12. William J. Baumol and William G. Bowen, *Performing Arts —
The Economic Dilemma* (New York: The Twentieth Century
Fund, 1966), p. 307.

13. *New York Times,* March 2, 1974.

14. *The Finances of the Performing Arts* (New York: Ford Foundation, 1974), p. 186.

CHAPTER 12. *Education's Insatiable Needs*

1. National Center for Educational Statistics, *Report for 1972–73*
(Washington, D.C.: Department of Health, Education and Welfare, 1973).

2. *Giving, USA 1974,* p. 25.

3. The facts in this paragraph come largely from Grace and Fred
M. Hechinger, *The New York Times Guide to New York City
Private Schools* (New York: Simon & Schuster, 1969).

4. James McLachlan, *American Boarding Schools* (New York: Charles Scribner's Sons, 1970), p. 3.
5. National Association of Independent Schools, Boston, February 1974.

Enrollment Patterns, 1968-69—1973-74
Percentage of increase or decrease over previous year

Schools	1968-69	1969-70	1970-71	1971-72	1972-73	1973-74
Girls' day	3.2	1.1	−0.4	−0.9	1.1	−0.6
Girls' boarding	1.4	−2.2	−2.9	−7.3	−1.7	−1.2
Boys' day	2.7	1.3	0.2	2.3	0.9	2.1
Boys' boarding	0.9	0.0	−3.3	−0.9	−0.1	−0.1
Co-educational day	4.3	2.7	3.1	3.0	3.8	1.1
Co-educational day elementary	6.9	5.5	8.5	2.4	1.6	2.8
Co-educational boarding	2.3	−0.2	−0.7	−2.0	1.7	2.6
Total enrollment, all schools	3.2	1.8	1.1	1.1	2.1	1.2

6. *New York Times*, December 4, 1970.
7. *New York Times*, January 30, 1971.
8. *New York Times*, February 22, 1971.
9. This analysis is largely taken from an article by Dr. Howard R. Bowen, Chancellor of Claremont College, in the *New York Times*, January 16, 1974.
10. Frank Bowles and Frank A. DeCosta, *Between Two Worlds — A Profile of Negro Higher Education* (New York: McGraw-Hill, 1971), chapter 9.
11. Rashi Fein and Gerald I. Weber, *Financing Medical Education* (New York: McGraw-Hill, 1971).

CHAPTER 13. *Racial Minorities*

1. For example: Charles Flint Kellogg, *NAACP — A History* (Baltimore: Johns Hopkins Press, 1967).
2. *New York Times*, November 11, 1974.
3. *Newsweek*, March 1, 1971.
4. Edgar S. Cahn, ed., *Our Brother's Keeper: The Indian in White America* (New York: World Publishing Co., 1969).

5. For a fuller discussion, see William Hosokawa, *Nisei, The Quiet Americans* (New York: William Morrow, 1969).
6. For detailed report, see *Wall Street Journal*, September 18, 1974.
7. Joan W. Moore, *Mexican Americans* (New York: Prentice-Hall, 1970), p. 52. See also *Business Week*, May 29, 1971.
8. Moore, *Mexican Americans*.
9. Alfredo Lopez, *The Puerto Rican Papers* (Indianapolis: Bobbs-Merrill Co., 1973), p. xii.

CHAPTER 14. *Saving Our Heritage for the Future*

1. Jeremy Main, "Conservationists at the Barricades," *Fortune*, February, 1970.
2. *New York Times*, June 27, 1974.
3. In an interview with Robert Reinhold, *New York Times*, August 10, 1969.
4. Diane K. Shah, "Safe, Studious Women Voters' League Takes up the Cudgels," *National Observer*, August 24, 1970.

CHAPTER 15. *Unmet Needs and Guides to Giving*

1. Alexis de Tocqueville, *Democracy in America*, vol. 1, ed. Phillips Bradley (New York: Alfred A. Knopf, 1948), p. 191.
2. For a detailed discussion of this major fraud see Scott M. Cutlip, *Fund Raising in the United States* (New Brunswick, N.J.: Rutgers University Press, 1965), pp. 461–69.

Selected Bibliography

A very complete and excellently compiled bibliography of virtually every book or article on the general subject of philanthropy exists under the title *Motivations for Charitable Giving* prepared in 1973 under the auspices of The 501(C)(3) Group, Suite 600, 1 Dupont Circle, N.W., Washington, D.C. 20036. Scholars and researchers can save considerable time in searching through library files by obtaining this modestly priced sixty-nine page pamphlet. In view of the comprehensiveness of this work, the following bibliography is limited to those titles I found most valuable on specific aspects of the subject.

GENERAL

Curti, Merle. *American Philanthropy Abroad: A History.* New Brunswick, N.J.: Rutgers University Press, 1963.
Cutlip, Scott M. *Fund Raising in the United States.* New Brunswick, N.J.: Rutgers University Press, 1965.
Owen, David. *English Philanthropy 1660 to 1960.* Cambridge, Mass.: Harvard University Press, Belknap Press, 1964.

TRUSTEES

Rauh, Morton A. *The Trusteeship of Colleges and Universities.* New York: McGraw-Hill, 1969.

FOUNDATIONS

Cuninggim, Merrimon. *Private Money and Public Service — The Role of Foundations in American Society*. New York: McGraw-Hill, 1972.
Goulden, Joseph C. *The Money Givers*. New York: Random House, 1971.
Nielsen, Waldemar A. *The Big Foundations*. New York: Columbia University Press, 1972.
Reeves, Thomas C., ed. *Foundations Under Fire*. Ithaca, N.Y.: Cornell University Press, 1970.

HISTORY OF AGENCIES

Dulles, Foster Rhea. *The American Red Cross, A History*. New York: Harper & Bros., 1950.
Hopkins, C. Howard. *History of YMCA in America*. New York: Association Press, 1951.
Oursler, Will. *The Boy Scout Story*. Garden City, N.Y.: Doubleday, 1955.

RELIGION

Cogley, John. *Catholic America*. New York: Dial Press, 1973.
Gollin, James. *Worldly Goods*. New York: Random House, 1971.
Lo Bello, Nino. *Vatican USA*. New York: Trident Press, 1972.

HOSPITALS

Greenberg, Selig. *The Quality of Mercy*. New York: Atheneum, 1971.
Somers, Herman Miles, and Somers, Anne Ramsay, *Medicare and the Hospitals: Issues and Prospects*. Washington, D.C.: The Brookings Institution, 1967.

CULTURE

Baumol, William J., and Bowen, William G. *Performing Arts — The Economic Dilemma*. New York: The Twentieth Century Fund, 1966.

Mayer, Martin. *Bricks, Mortar and the Performing Arts.* New York: The Twentieth Century Fund, 1970.

Reische, Dianah, ed. *The Performing Arts in America.* New York: H. W. Wilson Co., 1973.

Ripley, Dillon. *The Sacred Grove — Essays on Museums.* New York: Simon & Schuster, 1969.

Rockefeller Panel Report. *The Performing Arts — Problems and Prospects.* New York: McGraw-Hill, 1965.

EDUCATION

Barzun, Jacques. *The American University.* New York: Harper & Row, 1968.

Bowles, Frank, and DeCosta, Frank A. *Between Two Worlds — A Profile of Negro Higher Education.* New York: McGraw-Hill, 1971.

Cheit, Earl F. *The New Depression in Higher Education.* New York: McGraw-Hill, 1971.

Fein, Rashi, and Weber, Gerald I. *Financing Medical Education.* New York: McGraw-Hill, 1971.

McLachlan, James. *American Boarding Schools.* New York: Charles Scribner's Sons, 1970.

RACIAL MINORITIES

Cahn, Edgar S., ed. *Our Brother's Keeper: The Indian in White America.* New York: World Publishing Co., 1969.

Moore, Joan W. *Mexican Americans.* New York: Prentice-Hall, 1970.

Samora, Julian, ed. *La Raza: Forgotten Americans.* Notre Dame, Ind.: University of Notre Dame Press, 1966.

CONSERVATION

Adams, Alexander B. *Eleventh Hour — A Hard Look at Conservation,* New York: G. P. Putnam's Sons, 1970.

Index